'*Existential Therapy: Responses t*
is the perfect introduction to existe
cation to therapeutic practice and ε
experienced therapists, are to be congratulated for demystifying existential therapy. Their accessible, refreshingly jargon-free approach provides a companionable guide to this most practical of philosophies. While the Q&A format gives the reader the freedom to dip in and out, or read from cover-to-cover, as they please, it does not detract from the overall quality of the text. Anyone interested in the nature of human existence – whether trainee, practitioner, client, or the general reader – will find here inspiring and creative ways to meet the inevitable challenges of living.'

Simon du Plock, DCPsych, *Senior Research Fellow
at the Metanoia Institute, London*

'Existentialism has a reputation for being rather dense and consequently it is often misunderstood. This book shows that when written about well, its questions can become understandable, its insights can become practical and its relevance can become contemporary. The authors, all experts and teachers in the field, have distilled their experience and knowledge into a highly coherent and readable overview. Although written for relative beginners, it can offer a great deal to all readers whether familiar with existential therapy or not.'

Martin Adams, PhD, *author of* Skills in Existential
Counselling & Psychotherapy (with *E. van Deurzen*),
A Concise Introduction to Existential Counselling, *and*
An Existential Approach to Human Development

Existential Therapy

In *Existential Therapy: Responses to Frequently Asked Questions*, the authors address those questions most frequently asked by potential clients of existential therapy or by people beginning their training or by those interested in counselling or psychotherapy.

The book is divided into five parts, with each focusing on responding to questions about different elements of existential theory and its practice and applications:

- Part 1: Existential philosophy
- Part 2: Existential method and theory
- Part 3: Existential skills and practice
- Part 4: Existential applications in different contexts
- Part 5: Existential relevance to everyday life

The Q&A format, presented in an accessible language, emphasises commonly unknown or misunderstood areas that are typically overlooked.

The book will appeal to a wide audience of potential clients and trainees, practitioners from other approaches, and those outside of the profession who are curious to understand more about existential therapy.

Claire Arnold-Baker, Principal of NSPC and Director of Doctoral Programmes, is a counselling psychologist and existential psychotherapist with a small private practice where she specialises in working with mothers. Claire's previous publications include two edited books, and she co-authored *Existential Therapy: Distinctive Features*, with Emmy van Deurzen, as well as authoring other book chapters and journal articles.

Simon Wharne, DCPsych Deputy Course Leader at NSPC, is a counselling psychologist and existential psychotherapist with a small private practice. He has an interest in understanding neurodiversity and in supporting post-traumatic growth. Simon was formerly a manager in NHS mental health services, developing initiatives in assertive outreach and social inclusion. He has contributed book chapters and articles on these services, on resilience in mental health workers, and on hermeneutic phenomenological research methods.

Nancy Hakim Dowek, Foundation Course and DProf Programme Course Leader at NSPC, is an existential psychotherapist and supervisor in private practice. She has a special interest in transitional situations such as migration or life-limiting illnesses. Nancy has also authored a chapter in *Revisioning Existential Therapy* (edited by Mano Bazzano) and published articles based on her research on the experience of bi-rooted migrants.

Neil Gibson, Course Leader of the Existential Psychotherapy Training Programme at NSPC, is an existential psychotherapist and supervisor in private practice in Newcastle upon Tyne. Specialising these days in trauma, he has worked for over 20 years in the UK, Australia, and The Netherlands in different psychotherapy settings, including the NHS, universities, and various charitable organisations. He is currently chair of the UKCP Universities Training College, where he oversees the accreditation and regulation of university-based UK psychotherapy trainings.

Jo Molle, Coordinator of Masters Programmes at NSPC, is a chartered psychologist with a background in mental health research and has completed projects for various universities in the UK and the NHS. As a counsellor Jo is currently working in a low-cost community-based counselling service. Jo is also a departmental lecturer for the Department of Continuing Education at Oxford University.

Emmy van Deurzen, Founder and Director of NSPC, is an existential psychotherapist and counselling psychologist with a worldwide reputation. She has worked in the field for over 50 years and has published 18 books and hundreds of articles and chapters. Her work has been translated into countless languages, and she has lectured on six continents.

Edited by Windy Dryden, the *50 FAQs in Counselling and Psychotherapy Series* provides answers to questions frequently raised by trainees and practitioners in a particular area in counselling and psychotherapy.

Each book in the series is written by experts based on their responses to 50 frequently asked questions, divided into specific sections.

The series will be of interest to practitioners from all orientations including psychotherapists, clinical, health and counselling psychologists, counsellors, psychiatrists, clinically-oriented social workers and trainees in these disciplines.

Windy Dryden PhD is Emeritus Professor of Psychotherapeutic Studies at the Goldsmiths University of London. He is an international authority on Rational Emotive Behaviour Therapy and is in part-time clinical and consultative practice. He has worked in psychotherapy for more than 45 years and is the author and editor of over 250 books.

Single-Session Therapy: Responses to Frequently Asked Questions
By Windy Dryden

Pluralistic Therapy: Responses to Frequently Asked Questions
By Frankie Brown and Kate Smith

Acceptance and Commitment Therapy: Responses to Frequently Asked Questions
By Dawn Johnson and Richard Bennett

Existential Therapy: Responses to Frequently Asked Questions
By Claire Arnold-Baker, Simon Wharne, Nancy Hakim Dowek, Neil Gibson, Jo Molle with Emmy van Deurzen

Existential Therapy

Responses to Frequently Asked Questions

Claire Arnold-Baker,
Simon Wharne,
Nancy Hakim Dowek,
Neil Gibson, Jo Molle,
with Emmy van Deurzen

Routledge
Taylor & Francis Group

LONDON AND NEW YORK

First published 2024
by Routledge
4 Park Square, Milton Park, Abingdon, Oxon OX14 4RN

and by Routledge
605 Third Avenue, New York, NY 10158

Routledge is an imprint of the Taylor & Francis Group, an informa business

British Library Cataloguing-in-Publication Data
A catalogue record for this book is available from the British Library

ISBN: 9781032409887 (hbk)
ISBN: 9781032409856 (pbk)
ISBN: 9781003355700 (ebk)

DOI: 10.4324/9781003355700

Typeset in Times New Roman
by Newgen Publishing UK

This book is dedicated to lovers of
wisdom, wonder, and curiosity.

Contents

Part 2: Existential method and theory:
Questions about existential psychology and
psychotherapeutic work   35
NEIL GIBSON

Part 3: Existential skills and practice:
Questions about the way existential
therapists work   66
JO MOLLE

Introduction

Emmy van Deurzen

Existential therapy has become a well-established method of psychotherapy, which is now available widely across the world. It has deep roots in philosophy and can be traced back as far as the pre-Socratic search for a better way of life, as well as to the search for good living in many Eastern philosophies.

Existential therapy has been practised as a distinct form of psychotherapy for at least a century and started with the work of practitioners like Jaspers, Binswanger, Boss, and Frankl, who themselves were inspired by philosophers like Kierkegaard, Nietzsche, Husserl, Heidegger, Sartre, de Beauvoir, Merleau-Ponty, Camus, and many others. It has known a considerable increase in popularity over the past decades, and this is illustrated by the fact that there have been several hugely successful world congresses for existential therapy, in London, Buenos Aires, and Athens, in which therapists from all around the globe have come together to share their knowledge, wisdom, experience, and expertise. Some basic ideas from existential therapy are routinely taught in most counselling and psychotherapy training programmes. But nevertheless, existential therapy has remained puzzling or even obscured, to the wider public, and people continue to ask 'what does "existential" mean?' and 'how is existential therapy different to other forms of therapy?.'

This is the book that will answer all those questions you never dared to ask, lest you would appear to be ignorant. In these

DOI: 10.4324/9781003355700-1

pages you will find all the explanations you need, without the burden of complicated and intricate theorising. You will be able to get a grip on this unique approach, and hopefully this will spur you on to continue reading other books. You will discover some of the magic of existential work in completely down-to-earth words. You will realise how creative and productive this very pragmatic and yet deeply spiritual approach is. You will see that it is not necessary to speak about existential ideas in convoluted and knotty jargon, as there is a direct no nonsense way in which these issues can be approached. You will certainly find yourself drawn in to solving some of life's puzzles and become engaged with the process. You will soon get a sense of how all this is relevant to your own life and practice.

Existential therapists can be rather enigmatic at times, because most of the philosophers who inspired their work have written long and complex tomes about human existence that are dense and often difficult to understand. Human existence is not all that easy to fathom at the best of times, but it can get even more confusing when you face difficult trials and tribulations. It is all too easy to get stuck in the rabbit hole of your existential explorations. That is why it is vital that we can speak about these important matters without mystifying each other and without using knowledge in such a way that it perplexes people. We need clarity and practical wisdom because there is not much of it going spare in our materialistic societies.

It is therefore cause for great joy to see my colleagues and past trainees explain these complex issues in such elegant, direct, and vibrant ways, with practical examples and clear explanations. When I began to teach existential therapy in 1978, for the Arbours Association and Antioch University, London, nobody else was teaching existential ideas in the therapy world in the UK. I did not ever dream that the practice would become so widespread and well known, but all these decades later that is the situation. In those old days it was an uphill struggle to convince people that they could benefit from studying this subject and that their therapeutic work would benefit greatly. Some colleagues used to raise their eyebrows and enquire whether existentialism had not gone out of fashion. They thought it was a relic from the 1950s and 1960s and that it had passed its sell-by date. They could not have been more wrong. We are only at the start of the existential revolution that is so badly needed to clarify human existence in truthful and helpful ways and enable people to sort out their daily troubles. So many people are lost and confused or insecure or desperate. Coming to understand human existence has never gone out of fashion and never will. It is a long, winding, and unending road that we have to travel when figuring out how to live. The nineteenth- and twentieth-century philosophical movements of existentialism were just the forerunners of these investigations. There are now many new ways of working existentially, though they all share the same focus on elucidating human problems in living. Existential therapists go through a thorough training in philosophy, psychology, and psychotherapeutic skills. They learn about other modalities as well as doing an in-depth study of their own and their clients' struggles with human existence, before they begin their independent practice. Because existential therapy is a therapy that explores life in all its many facets, rather than a therapy that focuses mostly on a person's psyche, its range is very wide. There is a lot to learn and come to terms with.

One of the important elements of existential work is an awareness of connectivity, especially when working with people who are going through life transformations and crises that have knocked the stuffing out of them. At those times people have suffered important losses and that may feel very miserable and uncertain, because their framework of reference has been turned upside down and their worldview is in tatters. Rebuilding your understanding of life is best done by making sure to tackle the problems at all levels of existence, looking in the round at every experience and relationship, past, present, and future. To orientate yourself in life, you need to make strong connections to the physical world around you through your body and its senses. You also have to be fully engaged with your interpersonal relationships, figuring out what is going wrong with these and how you can improve them. Then you need to pay attention to your inner world and the way in which you relate to yourself and speak to yourself, often secretly. It matters greatly that you can create a thoughtful intimate world in which you feel at home and have a deep sense of integrity, peace, and respect for who you are. Finally, you cannot live a fulfilling life unless you are clearly and strongly in harmony with your values and have a sense of meaning and purpose in life.

This brings us to the importance of direction. To navigate through human existence, it helps to understand how the world works and figure out what role you can play in it. This means that you get a deep feeling of the things that matter to you and of the time that is available to you and how you wish to use it. Directing yourself through the four dimensions of the physical, the social, the personal, and the spiritual, is supplemented by becoming aware of the four dimensions of time: past, present, future, and eternity. Reflecting on how you spend your time on earth and how you manage the time available to you tends to bring a sense of urgency and awareness that you may not have acted in as much good faith and with as much care and compassion for yourself and others as you would like.

Another aspect of life that we often forget is that of conflict, dilemmas, contradictions, polarities, and paradoxes. Nothing is ever just one way or one sided and it is crucial that you learn to acknowledge the tensions, so that you can work with them, creating a wider life space for yourself. As long as you allow the world to oppress you, it is hard to engage with life. When you begin to understand how it works it becomes much easier to claim some freedom. Becoming more flexible, open minded, curious, willing to examine, explore, and investigate is what returns us to our safe harbour and allows us to set out on new adventures.

Tuning into our feelings and emotions is always the quickest way to begin that exploration of our existential path. For it is there that we encounter our own inclinations, desires, and motivations and that we retrieve the meanings that make sense of everything. If you want to tune into the world, you have to start by tuning in to yourself first. This book will definitely be a step in the right direction.

You can go to the questions that intrigue you most first, or you can read from cover to cover, to discover the full breadth of what is explained in the following pages. May your perambulations through the book bring you some valuable new insights and a lifelong taste for existential explorations.

Part 1

Existential philosophy

Questions about existential philosophical ideas

Claire Arnold-Baker

1.1 What is existentialism?

Existentialism is a branch of philosophy which concerns itself with understanding human existence. It considers such questions as 'what does it mean to be alive?,' 'why is there something rather than nothing?,' or 'what is the *Being* of human being?.' Existential philosophers have sought to uncover the essential structures of human existence that we all share and through this gain an understanding of what it means to be a human being.

Søren Kierkegaard (1813–1855) is often seen as the father of existentialism. During his brief life – he was 42 when he died – he was incredibly prolific, producing many philosophical works. What was distinctive about his work was its turn towards gaining an understanding of human existence, one of the first continental philosophers to do so at that time. Although it was Sartre's and Beauvoir's philosophical and literary works that brought existentialism into the mainstream and increased its popularity and visibility.

Warnock (1970) notes that the term *existentialist* was not one that was embraced by all philosophers who are defined as such today. She notes that despite this what unites existential philosophers was their interest in human freedom and human beings' ability to choose. This focus on free will makes existentialism a practical philosophy which, Warnock argues, gives

DOI: 10.4324/9781003355700-2

existentialism a 'missionary feel of conversion.' As in the process of becoming aware of freedom, individuals begin to see the world and themselves in a new way which cultivates a new attitude which can help them confront and address the problems they face in the world (Beauvoir, 2020).

The best-known existential philosophers are Kierkegaard, Nietzsche, Heidegger, Sartre, and Beauvoir. Kierkegaard highlighted the link between freedom and anxiety describing the 'dizziness of freedom' (1844, p. 61), a state of angst which emerges whenever individuals become aware of their freedom. This angst or anxiety emphasises that we always must choose how we live our lives, yet we only know the consequences of our choices in retrospect, and it is this aspect of choosing blindly that causes anxiety.

Nietzsche (1882), on the other hand, proclaimed that 'God is dead' and therefore without a higher power individuals are thrown back on themselves to create and recreate themselves.

Freedom was also a central aspect of Heidegger's (1927) concept of *authenticity*. If Dasein, or human *Being*, exists as possibility that is projected into the future, then how that possibility is grasped is connected to our freedom. When we act *authentically*, that is acting or being in accordance with what is good for us as an individual rather than falling in with others and society, then we are accessing our freedom to be ourselves.

These ideas were developed further by Sartre who stated that 'man was condemned to be free' (1943), which highlighted the burdensome nature of freedom, that it cannot be separated from our choices and subsequently the responsibility we hold for those choices.

Sartre noted that there were two types of existentialists, Christians and atheists; yet despite this difference he felt that all existential philosophers had in common the belief that '*existence* comes before *essence*' (1973, p. 26). This concept was central to Sartre's philosophical position on human existence, that 'Man is nothing else but that which he makes of himself. That is the first principle of existentialism' (ibid., p. 28). An idea echoed by Beauvoir who stated that 'the task of man is one: to fashion the world by giving it a meaning' (2020, p. 6).

It could be argued that existentialism is predominately Western as the existential philosophical movement developed in continental Europe during the twentieth century and its best-known philosophers are from this time and place. However, there are many more philosophers and thinkers who were interested in human existence and the human condition that preceded them. Greek philosophers such as Socrates, Plato, and Aristotle could be considered existential thinkers, as well as phenomenologists such as Husserl and Merleau-Ponty, theologians such as Tillich and Buber, and psychiatrists such as Jaspers, Boss, and Binswanger to name a few. There were also numerous other philosophers and writers; Dostoevsky is a good example of one of those who have written about existential ideas. Whilst these other writers and thinkers might not be considered existential philosophers who form part of the philosophical field of existentialism, their work contributes to the body of existential ideas from which existential therapy draws.

Existentialism has also suffered from criticism that it does not include any diverse thinkers and that existential philosophers were predominately white, Western men. Simone de Beauvoir was the notable exception, but more recently the work of Franz Fanon, a philosopher and psychiatrist, has become more recognised for his contribution to existential philosophy. There is also a parallel between existential ideas and those of eastern philosophy such as Buddhism, Taoism, and Confucianism. As Wang states 'Chinese literature resonates to a significant degree with Western existentialism' (2019, p. 579).

The twenty-first century has seen an interesting development in the field of existentialism, which has become split between an academic discipline of philosophy and an applied philosophy which forms the backbone of a therapeutic approach. Many of the new existential writers come from this applied field where they have gained rich insight into the human condition through their work with others.

1.2   What are the main themes of existential philosophy?

Human beings are paradoxical and complex and so any philosophy which aims to capture existence will, by necessity, be paradoxical too. There is no one way to live a life and no blueprint for living (Deurzen, 1988), therefore there can be no unified philosophy that will capture the entirety of human existence. This is highlighted in the works of existential philosophers who focused on different aspects of human existence and who sometimes took differing stances to each other in their theories and beliefs. Yet what unites existential philosophers is their focus on the aspects of existence that we all share, the underlying structures that make up our being. Some of the main themes of existential philosophy will be briefly summarised next to give a flavour of the shared aspects of our human existence.

Freedom, choice, and responsibility

As already seen in Section 1.1, all existential philosophers agree with the notion of freedom and that human beings have free will. This is an important idea in existential philosophy as it challenges notions of determinism that other therapeutic approaches uphold. Free will means that as individuals we have the freedom to choose how we respond to the challenges and accomplishments that life brings. It questions the notion of fate or other ways in which our lives might be directed by some higher being. If we have free will as human beings it means that everything must be chosen, how we respond to what happens to us, how we respond to others, but also how we respond to ourselves. All existential philosophers agree that we are the authors of our lives and ourselves, and that we must choose this every day. Therefore, freedom and choice are inextricably linked and both are tied together with responsibility. If we have free will and we choose ourselves and our lives then we must also take responsibility for what happens, and for the consequences of our choices. This is the burden that Sartre (1943) highlights in his philosophy.

Some may argue whether we do in fact have this level of free will when we live in societies which are structured by rules and expected ways of living. This type of absolute freedom is harder to achieve although not impossible. However, freedom is always within the limitations of our individual context and what is available to choose at any one time.

Kierkegaard (1844) noted that the difficulty that comes with our freedom to choose is that we cannot with any certainty know the outcome of our choices; there is no crystal ball that we can look into to see the future. The uncertainty caused by our own choices or the as yet unseen potential events or experiences that may befall us leads us to experience anxiety or *angst* as he termed it.

Death and anxiety

The fact that human beings have free will means that our natural human condition is one of anxiety. Another source of anxiety that human beings experience is that our lives are limited in time. It is the only certainty that we have in life – that we will die – but the time and manner of our death is unknown to us. This knowledge causes us to experience anxiety, anxiety over our choices and death anxiety over the ever-present possibility of our non-existence. To cope with this anxiety individuals try to tranquilise themselves by falling into everyday pursuits. However, Kierkegaard believed that our task was not to rid ourselves of the anxiety that living provoked or to try and deny it but rather see anxiety as a sign that we are alive and an opportunity to think about the choices that we are making to live a better life.

Existential guilt

When we are faced with needing to make a choice, there are always other choices that we have to reject and so we are forever in a situation where we are aware of both what we have chosen and what we have not. Existential guilt is therefore about what we have not done rather than feeling guilty about what we have done. This type of guilt relates to how we have not fulfilled our potential or lived true to ourselves. We feel guilty towards ourselves for what we have not done.

Authenticity and inauthenticity

Existential guilt is connected to inauthentic ways of being. Most of the time we live in inauthentic ways according to Heidegger (1927). We get caught up in everyday living and make choices that go along with others or society. Occasionally we feel the *call of conscience* which calls us to make choices that are good for us as an individual, we see our lives as a whole and in those moments we are authentic. But these are moments and quite quickly we fall back into more inauthentic ways of living.

The self

The existential view of the self is again different from other perspectives on the self. Existential philosophers do not see the self as something that is fixed and object like, instead they believed the self was more fluid and dynamic. We are becoming rather than something that can be easily defined and enduring. This sense of ourselves as always being in flux is another source of anxiety.

The absurd and meaning

When we think about our existence and how we are limited in time, life can feel absurd (Camus, 2000) and senseless. Yet Frankl (1946) stressed how we are meaning-creating beings and that our task in life is to create a life for ourselves despite its absurdity (Tillich, 1952).

Relationships with others

The final theme of existential philosophy is our interconnectedness with others and the world. Heidegger (1927) used the term *Being-in-the-World* to show how we are never isolated beings and that we are always in relation to other people and our surroundings.

1.3   Is existential therapy pessimistic?

Existential philosophy and therefore existential therapy have a reputation of being pessimistic. Having read through the main themes of existential philosophy in the previous question you may well agree with this view, especially as the focus of the philosophy and the therapy centres on ideas about death, anxiety, guilt, inauthenticity/authenticity, absurdity, and meaninglessness.

This, however, is not a new concern and one that has been levelled at existentialism in the past leading both Sartre and Beauvoir to counter it in their work. Beauvoir argued that

> Cut off from human will, the reality of the world is but an 'absurd given.' This is the conception that appears to many people as hopeless and makes them accuse existentialism of being pessimistic. But actually there is no helplessness, since we think that it is possible for man to snatch the world from the darkness of absurdity, clothe it in significations, and project valid goals into it.
>
> (2020, p. 6)

Sartre took a similar view when he stated that some

> ...complain that existentialism is too gloomy a view of things. Indeed their excessive protests make me suspect that what is annoying them is not so much our pessimism, but much more likely, our optimism.
>
> (1973, p. 25)

Both Sartre and Beauvoir highlight that the reality of our existence can be seen as challenging or even absurd, yet when we face these challenges something new opens up and we find possibilities that were not available to us before. For much of the time human beings try to turn themselves away from the possibility of their own death and the existential anxiety, guilt, and absurdity that is an inevitable part of human existence. Heidegger (1927) noted that people fall in with and go along with others as a way of avoiding confronting these realities of life. Yet if we face the possibility of our own death, for example, as an ever-present possibility, rather than being paralysed into inaction or getting caught up in morbid thoughts individuals are thrown back into their own life. If we only have a limited amount of time to live, then we are forced to think how we want to live our lives. Being limited in time makes us realise what is important and what we value. However, individuals tend to live without being conscious of time or how they are living their lives. They get shaken out of this reverie by moments of crisis, the death of another or the loss of a job or relationship or an accident happens which brings them back to the reality of their lives. It is at these moments that we can make active choices about how we want to live.

Therefore, rather than being at the mercy of things outside of our control, we have the possibility of making choices for ourselves and deciding the kind of life we want to live. Nietzsche (1882) had a similar view when he talked about the *eternal recurrence*, the idea that we should live each day as if we were living it for a second time and therefore becoming more acutely aware of *how* we are living and choosing in each moment rather than living our lives passively.

It follows then that rather than being pessimistic, existentialism is actually a more optimistic philosophy. It shows that despite the difficulties and hardships of life, the struggles and the absurdity that life brings, there are always ways in which we can make our lives significant and valuable and that this meaning is something that we ourselves can confer onto our lives. The attitude we take to life can determine the choices that we make and consequently the type of life we lead. But it takes courage, as Tillich (1952) reminds us, to be able to face these difficulties and continue in spite of them, to create a life for ourselves despite the fact that we will die. This is the rallying call of existentialism and what existential therapy helps clients to find for themselves.

1.4 What is the meaning of life?

Existential philosophy and therapy are associated with tackling the big questions of life. Perhaps the biggest question that has faced us, and one that human beings continually ask themselves, is what is the meaning of life? Questions about meaning have often revolved around whether there is one universal meaning to all of our lives or whether we each have to find our own personal meaning. Existential philosophers have largely posited the latter believing that there is no universal meaning, no celestial plan and instead individuals need to create their own meaning in life. Although they differ, however, in what they believe constitutes a meaningful life and how one might achieve one.

The challenge of finding a meaning in life is the absurdity of life itself. We are finite beings who have limited time, and our task, as Tillich (1952) proclaimed, is to have the courage to exist, or *Be*, and to create a life for ourselves in the face of non-being. Frankl (1946) believed that humans are intrinsically meaning-creating beings, that part of being human is that we create meaning from our experiences, a view similar to Beauvoir's (1947) idea that an aspect of our humanness is that we attribute value onto objects and experiences. It is up to us to decide what has value and what is important for us as an individual. Sartre concurred, objects in their own right do not hold any value, it is for us to give value to the things and people around us. In fact, Beauvoir believed that the way in which we counter the absurdity of life is that we only pursue projects that do hold value for us; we do not engage in projects that have no value for us.

These ideas around value are linked to the second aspect of meaning which is a sense of purpose. Most existential philosophers describe meaning in life in terms of what we are directed towards. For Nietzsche, we create meaning through moving from one goal to another and that meaning in life is a life-long project of self-creation and recreation. Meaning comes through our creativity, our emotions, and our passions. Nietzsche saw the art of creativity as one which involves self-reflection and self-exploration. Creativity is not just about producing something that is original, but the process of creativity changes the individual, as Belliotti explains 'Creative activity spawns self-transformation' (2018, p. 187). Sartre not only saw how meaning came through our daily pursuits but also believed that we were guided in our pursuits by what he called the 'original project,' an idea or ideal that we move towards. Similarly, Beauvoir describes how our human agency pulls us towards what we want to achieve because the end of the project is valuable to us. As one project ends it forms the basis or foundations of the next project we move onto and in this way our life moves forward with direction and intention.

This idea that what we turn our attention to, what projects we engage in, is also important in how we develop as individuals. The projects that we pursue are meaningful because we give them value, but in the process of pursuing them we change something of ourselves and therefore gain a sense of being meaningful as well as leading meaningful lives. This is most keenly seen in Kierkegaard's work. Kierkegaard boldly stated that 'the thing is to find a truth that is truth *for me*, to find *the idea for which I am willing to live and die*' (1835, p. 75). This question 'what should I live for?' becomes the central question of Kierkegaard's philosophy. Kierkegaard's views differ from other existential philosophers as he believes that meaning ultimately comes through a leap of faith towards God. Yet his initial question 'what should I live for?' and his ideas about the task of life is one of developing ourselves as individuals are echoed by other philosophers such as Heidegger. Heidegger (1927) does not directly discuss meaning in life in his books, although it is implicit in his philosophy and his ideas around authenticity and inauthenticity, where meaningfulness is connected to authenticity. He believed that when we live in an inauthentic way, we are trying to flee from ourselves and ultimately death. However, when we accept the finitude of existence that our life is limited and therefore precious, we make choices that determine who we are going to be. To be authentic is therefore to live in accordance with those choices and to make choices that are good for us as an individual and which will fulfil our potential. Living authentically then gives purpose and direction to life.

Camus (2000) looked at meaning indirectly by exploring absurdity and meaninglessness. His most famous example is the myth of Sisyphus, which tells of a mortal who is punished by the Gods into pushing a boulder up a hill and when at the top it rolls back down again, and he must repeat this for eternity. Camus questioned whether such a meaningless task can ever be meaningful. Yet in the end he argues that Sisyphus makes the task *his* task, takes ownership of the project he has been set, and gives value to what he is doing. Thereby demonstrating that even things that seem meaningless can become meaningful. These ideas were also taken up by Frankl who believed that suffering ceases to be suffering when it becomes meaningful.

The meaning of life for existential philosophers and therapists is that there is no one meaning that is universal to all, although Sartre did believe that individual meaning can reveal the meaning of existence for all humanity. Rather meaning is more individual to each person's life and how that person ascribes value to what they do and believe. Meaning in life does not have to be one all-encompassing thing that we have to search for. Instead, it is found in everyday pursuits and the achievement of completing projects or the process of being creative. Meaning in life comes from the attitude we take to our lives and in particular the attitude we take to the suffering and despair that we feel. An aspect that Kierkegaard felt was essential before we could take the 'leap of faith' we needed to have accepted and embraced our own suffering, despair, and sadness. A meaningful life also comes from a sense of purpose and direction, reconnecting to our 'original project' and living in accordance with who we are. To find out what is important and meaningful for us we need to ask ourselves 'what should I live for?.'

1.5   Does existential philosophy only focus on the present?

Existential philosophers are mainly interested in discovering the fundamental ontological structures of human existence that we all share. In other words, they are concerned with uncovering what makes us human and highlighting what elements are universal to all regardless of culture or religion. The focus therefore is not so much about the present moment as such but rather how we can understand human *Being*. Existential philosophers, especially Heidegger, felt that you cannot understand human existence without examining how we live in time, temporality. Heidegger (1927) devoted the second half of his book *Being and Time* to the subject and emphasised its importance on our existence. He dismissed a more linear description of time and believed that the past is carried into the present moment and both of which are projected into the future. Therefore, the present moment at any one time contains both the past and the future within it. An illustration of the Dialectic of Time (DoT), a development of Heidegger's work, can be found in Deurzen and Arnold-Baker's (2018) book, *Existential Therapy: Distinctive Features*. The DoT demonstrates how these three temporal *ectasies*, as Heidegger (1927) describes them, interplay with a fourth temporal element, that of the eternal.

This view of temporality is important for existential therapy as it provides a new way of understanding human experience. Looking at temporality through this lens means that our past does not determine who we are but rather the past is alive in the present moment. Although we cannot change what has happened to us in the past, we are able to choose how we remember or recollect it or how we make sense of those past experiences. Similarly, our past experiences do not need to impact our future choices, the future is open for us to choose differently if we have the courage to do so. This allows us freedom although as previously described in Section 1.2, this freedom comes with choice and responsibility. Thoughts about our future can in turn influence the present moment and how we think about or the attitude we take towards past events. Temporality therefore highlights the dynamic nature of human existence. Nothing stands still, our past is active in the present, the future is open before us, and both past and future can influence how we live in the present moment. This can be incredibly freeing as a notion but also provoke feelings of anxiety and uncertainty if everything is so subject to flux.

As Heidegger rightly pointed out, human existence is tied to two temporal markers, our birth and our death; they are the only certainties in life: that once we are born, we will die. They are both boundary points to non-existence, we come from non-existence through conception and birth and return to non-existence in death. Both natality and mortality have profound implications for how our existence is structured. Whilst much has been written from an existential perspective about the impact mortality has on how we live our lives, it is only more recently that Arendt's (1998) work on natality has been taken up by Stone (2019) to examine the impact that our birth also has on our lives.

Stone highlights that the very act of being born sets in motion certain structures and constraints to our existence. We are born vulnerable, and this therefore demonstrates the *dependency* we have on others, right from the start of life. Other people can be our saviours or our tormentors but either way we must learn how to relate to others. For Stone this is our *relationality*, another aspect of human *Being* that is present at the start which links with Heidegger's view that we exist as *Being-with*. The other two ways in which natality structures our human condition, according to Stone, are connected to Heidegger's idea of *Thrownness*. At birth we are *thrown*/born into the world to parents, country, culture, religion, and situation. These aspects cannot be chosen and represent the givens of our lives. They represent our *situatedness*, the context in which we live which also includes *social power relations* that exist within that situation. What is interesting is how the two ends of our lives structure our lives in opposing ways. Natality emphasises our relationality and dependency on others, whereas mortality emphasises our individuality and uniqueness.

These two poles of our existence will of course be present in any moment and how we experience our lives will also be down to the structures created by our human condition. The dynamic nature of our lives means that a focus on the present also brings in the past and the future as it is experienced in that present moment. It allows individuals to take stock of their lives (Deurzen, 1988), to check on where they are in their lives in the temporal sphere between birth and death. To reflect on the impact of the past, what stops them potentially moving forward in a different way into the future or how do they want to move into that future? These are the questions that life demands we consider and ones that become the mainstay of existential therapy. Human agency always pulls us forward into our lives, Heidegger talks about human *Being* as one of projection. The question then is how one moves forward, and this is also linked to meaning and purpose which is discussed further in Section 1.4.

1.6   Is existentialism more about individuals than societies?

One of the core ideas of existential philosophy is freedom (see Section 1.1), that individuals have *free will* to create and recreate themselves and their lives. This often leads to a misconception that existential philosophy is individualistic, that the focus is on how each person enacts their *free will* or freedom to enable them to find meaning and purpose in life and to move towards more authentic ways of being. These ideas are, of course, all present in existential philosophy and are a main component of existential thinking. We are only ever able to effect or change ourselves and yet as individuals we have an impact on others and the world around us.

However, as mentioned in Section 1.5, human beings are intrinsically relational, *Being-with* as Heidegger (1927) terms it, which is a fundamental aspect of the human condition. Human beings start life relationally rather than individually, completely dependent on others for their basic needs and survival. A sense of becoming an individual develops over time, according to Sartre, when a child starts to recognise themselves as separate and get a sense of 'me, not me' (Barnes, 1990).

As individuals we are never in isolation; we are always in relation, both to ourselves and to other people and the world around us. Heidegger (1927) uses the term *Being-in-the-World* to demonstrate this interconnection. Human existence is paradoxical and one of the tensions we must hold is between individuality and relationality. How can we hold onto a sense of ourselves as an individual when we are always part of a larger society and culture? How can we consider the impact that we have on others and others have on us in the knowledge that we are vulnerable and dependent on others? We cannot act in isolation; our actions will always have some impact on those around us and the world that we are living in. This aspect highlights the limitations of our freedom and *free will*. Individuals can choose to act in a way that benefits them as an individual, but this means taking responsibility for the consequences of those actions. That is the burden of freedom that Sartre (1943) emphasises in his work. Beauvoir (2004) added a moral dimension to her philosophical ideas about how human beings pursue meaning through under-taking tasks whose ends are meaningful to the individual. She warns, however, that it can only be meaningful if it does not 'harm' another person.

Each existential philosopher takes a slightly different pos-ition on the relationships we have with others. Heidegger (1927) talks about how we become *fallen in* with others, becoming part of an anonymous 'They,' and are taken over by what 'The They' thinks and believes. Going along with others helps tranquilise individuals from the anxiety that they would experience if they became truly aware of their existence, the recognition that they are limited in time and will die and that they have a need to choose a life for themselves. Although, he believed that there are times when we are able to separate and think of ourselves as individuals, which enables us to make choices that are right for us, and in those moments moving into a more authentic way of living. Heidegger's ideas about 'The They' are similar to Nietzsche's (1973) 'The Herd' or herd mentality, where people go along with the crowd and are scared to stand out. Nietzsche cautions the negative impact others can have on an individual and how it is important for each of us to create space for our-selves and create lives of our own rather than being taken over by what others think and do.

The negative impact people have on each other was perhaps most famously captured by Sartre who stated, 'Hell is other people' (1949, p. 57). Sartre's examination of human relationships concluded that each individual is trying to enact their freedom within a relationship and therefore in the process it reduces the other into an object. He describes 'the look' where we become aware of the gaze of the other and how in that moment, we have become objectified in their eyes, causing a sense of shame and judgement. Sartre's view of relationships has a feeling of being combative and competitive where each party tries to gain control over the other in various ways. Although Sartre's later work does acknowledge that positive relationships can be possible and that these are based on generosity towards the other which brings mutuality. An idea echoed by Merleau-Ponty who noted the reciprocal nature of human relationships particularly regarding our bodily experience. Merleau-Ponty (1962) describes how in the same instant that we touch another we are touched. Sartre's later ideas were also influenced by his relationship with Beauvoir and her views on relationships. Beauvoir (1949) took a slightly different view in looking at how in heteronormative relationships the woman is often seen as 'other' thus creating an unequal relationship. She believed that more equal relationships can be attained through collaboration and cooperation.

Buber (1970) probably gives the most positive view of the potential of our relationships with others. Whilst he recognises that for a lot of the time individuals treat others in an *I-It* way, reducing them to objects in the way Sartre describes. He does also acknowledge that there are moments of what he calls *I-Thou*, where each person is truly connecting with the other with the whole of themselves. They are completely with the other in those moments, not trying to get anything from the other, or trying to understand them, just *being with* them.

An existential view of relationships highlights the complex interplay of tensions, between being an individual and being part of a society. It can help us think about how we can respond to the fact that we are intrinsically dependant on others, and that we cannot live separately from others, and therefore, relationships based on generosity and mutuality will serve us better than those based on fear and control.

1.7   What is an existential crisis?

Until recently an *existential crisis* was a relatively unknown term restricted to existential psychotherapeutic literature. But increasingly it is a term that has become part of our common parlance. Deurzen (2021) describes how it has been bandied about by politicians, journalists, or business owners to describe a risk or a threat to a person or an organisation. This has the effect of placing an emphasis of an existential crisis on mortality and non-existence rendering the term synonymous with a fear of death, destruction, or devastation. Whereas an existential crisis is more broadly related to how we experience or are confronted by our existence in general.

Heidegger (1927) highlighted how as human beings we mainly exist as *fallenness*. That we fall in with others and their ways of being and we become *tranquilised* towards our existence and the way we are living our lives. We engage in this way of being, Heidegger argues, to protect ourselves from the anxiety that would be evoked if we were confronted by the reality of our existence and what it would mean for our lives. We live in a way where we feel we have some control over our lives, that our lives and our relationships will follow predictable paths and that our values and beliefs about the world and ourselves are stable and based on our experiences and knowledge. When we are confronted by an existential crisis, we begin to see the reality of our existence more clearly. We see how things that we have held to be true can be challenged and the security that we felt can be taken from us and where we are confronted by the unpredictable nature of life. Heidegger (1927) describes this experience as *umheimlich*, or of being 'not-at-home' in our lives, it is an unsettling feeling.

The *crisis*, of an existential crisis, emphasises how abruptly it can occur in a person's life. A sudden change, when something unexpected happens, that has the effect of disrupting a person's life completely. These situations can feel as if everything has been thrown up in the air and it is difficult to see how it will land and the impact it will have. Often these life crises are just that, times of personal crisis, be it a conflict, illness, bereavement, redundancy, or divorce, for example. Or the crisis may affect more people at the same time such as a global health pandemic or it can be geo-political in nature such as Brexit, climate change, or war (Deurzen, 2021). All these events happen suddenly or in a short space of time and have the effect of leaving a person feeling untethered to their lives. However, other life events that seem less dramatic can also lead to an existential crisis, such as midlife, retirement, or motherhood (Arnold-Baker, 2020). These life crises bring their own difficulties as, although they are expected, and in some cases longed for, they can still bring about significant changes to how a person experiences themselves and their lives.

An existential crisis has the ability of shining a light on our lives and we become more aware of how our life is structured in existential ways. Birth and death are important temporal markers, but equally important is how we relate to our freedom, choice, responsibility, meaning, identity, and value. All of these are aspects of human *Being* for which we are required to take a stance. We must choose how we live despite knowing that we will one day die – how we make choices, how we enact our freedom, how we take on responsibility, and how we create a sense of identity, meaning, and value in our life. This can often feel a burdensome task, or it is one we have not engaged with actively as we have gone along with our lives.

When we examine the etymology of the word *crisis*, it comes from the Greek word *Krisis*, which means to choose or to decide (Arnold-Baker, 2020; Deurzen, 2021). Therefore, an existential crisis might more accurately be described as a situation that urgently requires us to become aware of, and to make choices about, our existence. An existential crisis provokes a question, and we must answer it in how we think about and live our life. It may mean that we have to rethink our embodiment and how we are physically connected to our lives and where we can feel safe. Our relationships may also be called into question leading us to consider who we can trust and where we belong. The crisis might make us question ourselves, who we are now in light of this new event or situation. How our identity has to adapt to make room for this new reality. Finally, how we make sense of the existential crisis will affect what we value and believe and what is meaningful for us and ultimately where our purpose lies. Most existential crises will impact all four dimensions of existence (Arnold-Baker, 2020): the physical, social, personal, and spiritual.

The choices that an existential crisis calls for are not easily or quickly made, however. It takes time to make sense of and assimilate what has happened into a person's life. To start with, a person might just feel in shock or in trauma about how much their life has changed. There might be feelings of grief over the loss of their previous way of living, or anger at the unfairness of the world and actions of others. But if time is taken to address what has happened and attention given to the existential questions that have arisen, then a transformation can occur. Individuals can begin to live their lives in more meaningful and purposeful ways. Fundamentally an existential crisis will cause a change in how a person sees themselves, their lives, and the world, but the process of confronting existence with courage brings with it wisdom and learning that will lead to better ways of living.

1.8   Can existentialism exist alongside religious beliefs?

Existential philosophers can broadly be divided into those who have a belief in God and those who are atheists. Nietzsche famously proclaimed that 'God is dead' which meant that if there is no God then individuals need to create their own values and beliefs to live by. An idea taken up by the French existential philosophers. But it raises questions about whether a belief in God is compatible with a belief that as human beings we have *free will*. Kierkegaard's view was that there are different *stages of life*, the final stage being where an individual would live a religious life and create a relationship with God. However, this stage was not the one that can be cultivated or that one can just decide to have. For Kierkegaard faith was more important than belief. He believed that creating a relationship with God was only possible through taking a risk and allowing doubt, sin, and suffering into a person's life. Through opening yourself up in this way Kierkegaard saw that individuals could then take a *leap of faith*, out into the world and towards God. *Free will* for Kierkegaard would centre on an individual's ability to choose to create a direct relationship with God. Tillich (1952) had a similar view to Kierkegaard in that he believed relating to God 'was the only way to fully *be*' (Deurzen & Kenward, 2005). Although he argued against the notion of one God and saw God as a symbol of ultimate authority and reality. Both philosophers were interested in how we relate to something beyond ourselves and the world, rather than putting the focus on organised religion as such.

There are, of course, many systems of belief and religion across the world. Religious beliefs can be considered one way of making sense of and understanding the world that we live in. It is one way in which individuals can relate to the fact that there are things about existence that we do not know. Religion also gives people an overarching worldview, a code of ethics and morals and a system to live by. Religious beliefs like any system of beliefs need not only to be understood and articulated but also to be examined so that they do not become set in stone (Deurzen, 2010) and followed doggedly, which means that new ways of thinking and living are not entertained.

There are elements of some religious beliefs that do not sit well with existential thought, especially ideas about creation and what happens after a person dies. Other ideas that are incompatible with notions of free will are that events or things happen because of 'God's will.' These beliefs go against an existential view that human existence is based on freedom to choose and an individual's ability to create and recreate a life for themselves. Nietzsche's concern was that if God could no longer be relied upon, morality and value in life would be lost which would have implications for society and the way in which individuals live.

One way of looking at religion is that it offers individuals a way of making sense of and meaning out of an existence that often feels meaningless. It provides a moral and ethical code and ascribes values to live by. Existential philosophers would argue that these elements need to be created by human beings rather than Gods and that this is our task in life. This does not mean that a spiritual dimension cannot be created but it would be found, as Kierkegaard (1835) demanded, through an idea that a person is willing to live and die for.

A spiritual dimension to human existence, therefore, concerns our understanding of the world, but it also extends to how we relate to time and the temporal dimension of the eternal, as well as how we relate to the metaphysical dimension of being, that of the unknown. When we ask questions about how do we come to exist? Or why is there being rather than non-being? Then we are engaging in questions about spirituality. The important aspect is to engage in dialogue rather than dogmatism and to allow for openness so that beliefs can be re-evaluated over time. In this way different beliefs and values can exist alongside each other in authentic ways.

1.9 Does existential philosophy encompass all aspects of human existence?

Existential philosophy is primarily concerned with understanding the nature of being. It can be seen as a branch of philosophy called metaphysics, which considers the question of whether human beings exist at all. Existential philosophers, however, agree that human beings *do* exist and therefore their preoccupation is on the structure or conditions of that existence or *being*. This aspect is often described as ontological, and existential philosophers seek to uncover, or disclose, the fundamental aspects that are universal to all, or as Aristotle describes, the essential essences of human being (Deurzen & Kenward, 2005, p. 146). Heidegger's (1927) book *Being and Time* is devoted to describing the ontology of *Being* setting out to describe the structures that make up the *Being* of human beings. Heidegger uses phenomenology as a method by which he undertakes this examination (phenomenology is described further in Section 2.3) and uses the term *Dasein* to mean being-there.

All the main existential thinkers are concerned with ontology in varying different ways, and how human beings are becoming rather than fixed entities. Some of the ontological features of human *being* have already been described in previous questions, such as freedom, choice, responsibility, anxiety, mortality, natality, and guilt. These are the aspects that all human beings face as part of their humanness. However, existential philosophers, such as Heidegger, tend not to explore what they would term the ontic experience of these ontological conditions, that is how we might experience or make sense of these aspects. Deurzen and Kenward define ontic as 'ontic investigation is concerned with particular beings or things (*existents*), as they are actually manifest in the world, beings whose existence is taken for granted' (2005, p. 146). For example, freedom is an ontological condition of human existence, yet how an individual experiences that freedom is an ontic expression.

Therefore, the ontic is about the concrete facts of human existence, that is those things that we can obverse and investigate. It therefore follows that existential philosophy does not encompass all ontic expressions and areas that would make up psychology as a discipline and which are the focus of an existential therapeutic approach.

Existential philosophy does not have a theory of mind for example or of personality. Existential philosophy would not seek to divide individuals into 'types,' where each 'type' has a state or a trait. As this would suggest that human beings have a self that is fixed and object-like that can be described and classified. Instead, existential philosophers see human beings as *becoming* or potential, an ever-changing and dynamic process that is projected forward into the world through freedom. Sartre (1943) took this further to suggest that human beings are essentially nothingness and through their existence they create a sense of themselves, but this sense is fluid and open to change. Existential philosophy also does not provide a map or blueprint (Deurzen, 1988) for how one should live their life; there is no ideal way of living.

Existential philosophy also does not expound a theory of human development as this suggests that there is a 'self' to develop or that there are specific ways in which human beings change over the lifespan. This does not mean, however, that existential philosophers do not think that individuals change, quite the contrary, as change is an essential aspect of human existence. Existential philosophers, however, would disagree that there are set stages that all human beings go through over the lifetime at particular ages or times. The type of 'development' that existential philosophers describe is how individuals become more aware of themselves as individuals, how particular experiences in life become transformational as they serve as moments for individuals to stop and reflect on their lives and to have the opportunity to make choices that are considered more authentic and good for them (Adams, 2018).

Kierkegaard's (1843) *stages of life* and Nietzsche's (1883) *three metamorphoses of the spirit* are attempts by the philosophers to demonstrate how individuals might develop and reach their potential and the stages they need to go through in order to do that. Although there is no consensus between them of what this potential might be or indeed any agreement of the stages required.

1.10 Do clients need to know anything about existential philosophy?

Existential therapy often has an aura of mystery surrounding it. Many potential clients are not familiar with the term or have not heard about the approach as it is not as mainstream as other approaches to therapy such as psychoanalysis or Cognitive Behavioural Therapy (CBT). Therefore, potential clients may be unsure of what a philosophical approach might entail and whether this is something that would be helpful for them or one they would need. In recent years the approach has gained more visibility (Deurzen et al., 2019) and indeed the term 'existential' has been used more widely by the media when talking about seismic events that have happened or are happening, such as climate change or other events which seem to denote a threat or a risk to human existence or the existence of an organisation.

Some clients may choose to have existential therapy specifically and feel that a philosophical approach is more aligned with how they understand their problems and with their values and beliefs, but for a lot of clients they may be unaware of the approach and what it entails. One of the main questions people ask is whether you must know anything about existential philosophy in order to have existential therapy and the short answer is 'no you don't.'

Existential philosophy is the foundation from which existential therapists understand the world and other people. When a therapist takes a philosophical rather than a psychological view to human suffering, they focus on the struggles people face in living rather than seeing those difficulties stemming from a psychological or biological nature. Viewing people's issues as difficulties in living means that the focus is put not only on how individuals are in the world, how they act and interact with it and others around them but also on how they relate to themselves. A philosophical approach sees individuals as being part of a complex web of connections and that these different connections contribute to the difficulties they experience in their lives. If a person is suffering from depression for example, a philosophical perspective would look at the ways in which the person has become disconnected from their lives in various ways or how they are experiencing the world whilst feeling depressed.

An existential therapist will also use existential philosophy to help them understand their clients and their concerns which will inform the focus of the therapy and how they respond. Inevitably as part of the therapy, therapists will be aware of existential themes that might be present for the client, such as how clients experience their freedom, what are the choices they are making, and how are they accepting responsibility in their lives. Other themes concern mortality, meaning, temporality, etc. These are all ontological conditions (see Section 1.9) that we all face as human beings.

Of course, clients in existential therapy will not be overtly aware of these aspects. Existential therapists do not talk to their clients directly about philosophy or how they can understand their struggles philosophically. The dialogue remains very much at the ontic level (experience level) of the client's experience. Some clients may wish to talk about philosophical issues and for those clients the therapist would always bring the client back to their own life experience, how the issue that they are wanting to discuss relates to their own lives and what meaning it holds. Staying at a philosophical level will not help the client to understand what has gone wrong in their life and how they might live better.

However, an existential approach to therapy does have a direct philosophical aspect as it invites clients to be curious and questioning about their lives. The term *Philosophy* comes from the Greek words '*philo*' and '*sofia*' meaning 'love of wisdom,' and it is this search for wisdom that is an intrinsic part of existential therapy. Therefore, although clients are not expected to know any existential philosophy, they will be expected to think deeply about their lives and the way they are living. The aim of therapy is not for therapists to give clients answers to their problems, and the goal is not to seek solutions as such, but rather to engage in a deep reflection which enables clients to examine what is important in their lives. A goal of existential therapy would be to start a journey to find a better way of living.

When the focus changes to how can we live in a better way, it may turn the discussion towards looking at 'big philosophical questions,' such as 'what is the meaning of life?' (see Section 1.4). But these questions would always be generated by the client and discussed in relation to the client's life and their worldview. Existential therapists do not turn away from more challenging areas such as death or the absurdity of life if raised by, or relevant to, what the client is bringing. They will draw on their understanding of existence from existential philosophy to guide their interventions and questions, with the aim of not wanting to calm or tranquilise the client and ease their anxiety but rather help the client to confront these essential aspects of life and how they can live well in spite of them.

Further reading

Adams, M. (2018). *An Existential Approach to Human Development: Philosophical and Therapeutic Perspectives*. Red Globe Press.

Deurzen, E. van & Arnold-Baker, C. (2018). *Existential Therapy: Distinctive Features*. Routledge.

Leach, S. & Tartaglia, J. (Eds.) (2018). *The Meaning of Life and the Great Philosophers*. Routledge.

Warnock, M. (1970). *Existentialism*. OPUS.

References

Adams, M. (2018). *An Existential Approach to Human Development: Philosophical and Therapeutic Perspectives*. Red Globe Press.

Arendt, H. (1998). *The Human Condition*. University of Chicago Press.

Arnold-Baker, C. (Ed.) (2020). *The Existential Crisis of Motherhood*. Palgrave Macmillan.

Barnes, H. (1990). Sartre's concept of the self. In K. Hoeller (ed.) *Sartre and Psychology*. Humanities Press (1993).

Beauvoir, S. de (1947). *What Is Existentialism?* Penguin (2004).

Beauvoir, S. de (1949). *The Second Sex*. Vintage Classics (1997).

Belliotti, R.A. (2018). Nietzsche and the meaning of life. In S. Leach & J. Tartaglia (Eds.), *The Meaning of Life and the Great Philosophers*. Routledge, 182–190.

Buber, M. (1970). *I-Thou* (W. Kaufmann, trans.). Charles Scibner's.

Camus, A. (2000). *The Myth of Sisyphus* (J. O'Brien, trans.). Penguin Classic.

Deurzen, E. van (1988). *Existential Counselling in Practice*. Sage.

Deurzen, E. van (2010). *Everyday Mysteries: A Handbook of Existential Psychotherapy*. Routledge.

Deurzen, E. van (2021). *Rising from Existential Crisis: Life Beyond Calamity*. PCCS Books.

Deurzen, E. van & Arnold-Baker, C. (2018). *Existential Therapy: Distinctive Features*. Routledge.

Deurzen, E. van, Craig, E., Längle, A., Schneider, K.J., Tantam, D. & du Plock, S. (2019). *The Wiley World Handbook of Existential Therapy*. Wiley Blackwell.

Deurzen, E. van & Kenward, R. (2005). *Dictionary of Existential Psychotherapy and Counselling. Sage Publications*.

Frankl, V. (1946). *Man's Search for Meaning*. Washington Square Press (1984).

Heidegger, M. (1927). *Being and Time* (J. Macquarrie & E.S. Robinson, trans.). Harper and Row (1962).

Kierkegaard, S. (1835). *Søren Kierkegaard's Journals and Papers.* Indiana University Press.

Kierkegaard, S. (1843). *Either/Or: A Fragment of Life* (A. Hannay, trans.). Penguin (1992).

Kierkegaard, S. (1844). *Concept of Anxiety* (R. Thomte, trans.). Princeton University Press.

Merleau-Ponty, M. (1962). *The Phenomenology of Perception* (C. Smith, trans.). Routledge (1998).

Nietzsche, F. (1882). *The Gay Science* (W. Kaufmann, trans.). Vintage Books (1974).

Nietzsche, F. (1883). *Thus Spoke Zarathrustra* (R.J. Hollingdale, trans.). Penguin (1961).

Nietzsche, F. (1973). *The Will to Power in Science, Nature, Society and Art.* Random House.

Sartre, J-P. (1943). *Being and Nothingness: An Essay on Phenomenological Ontology* (H. Barnes, trans.). Philosophical Library.

Sartre, J-P. (1949). *No Exit and Three Other Plays.* Vintage Books.

Sartre, J-P. (1973). *Existentialism & Humanism.* Methuen.

Stone, A. (2019). *Being Born: Birth and Philosophy.* Oxford University Press.

Tillich, P. (1952). *The Courage to Be.* Yale University Press.

Wang, X. (2019). An east-west dialogue: An outline of existential therapy development in China and related Asian countries. In E. van Deurzen et al. (Eds.), *The Wiley World Handbook of Existential Therapy.* Wiley, 579–591.

Warnock, M. (1970). *Existentialism.* OPUS.

Part 2

Existential method and theory

Questions about existential psychology and psychotherapeutic work

Neil Gibson

2.1 Do existential therapists get you to think about death?

An existential psychotherapist will approach their client's difficulties without a set agenda. A client who comes to therapy may not be dwelling on their inevitable death and indeed the topic of their mortality (or anyone else's) may never, explicitly at least, be broached. Some existential psychotherapists, such as Irvin Yalom, believe that death awareness is the foundation on which an effective approach to psychotherapy is constructed. He notes that 'although the physicality of death destroys man, the idea of death saves him' (Yalom, 1980, p. 30). It is, you might say, the bottom line.

People bring all manner of emotional and psychological problems into the consulting room and it is the existential therapist's job to help bring clarity and understanding to their situation so that they can become more authentically engaged in the living of their life, with more awareness of the extent of their freedom and choice. It is impossible, however, to live without eventually dying, and so death is inevitably the backdrop to every decision or action we take. It is there all the time. Although this is a simple and perhaps obvious truth, it is nonetheless profound because it is through our awareness of our inevitable demise that our existence is put into stark relief,

DOI: 10.4324/9781003355700-3

rendering our life simultaneously meaningful and meaningless. Existential psychotherapist, Emmy van Deurzen, describes the tension between birth and death:

> Birth and death are like the horizon of our sheer earthly existence: the parameters against which our living is enacted... Life is the tension between coming into the world and going out of it again... It is only to be expected that both [birth and death] remind us of our humble and fragile nature. When the mystery of birth or death does touch us, we are inevitably altered in this process.
>
> (Deurzen-Smith, 1997, p. 105)

So, what is the significance of death to the everyday practice of psychotherapy, and how is death manifest in the therapeutic process? To understand this, we shall need to now turn to the two main players: anxiety and authenticity.

> We all know that in the basic boundaries of existence we are no different from others. No one at a conscious level denies that. Yet, deep, deep down, each of us believes..., that the rule of mortality applies to others but certainly not to ourselves.
>
> (Yalom, 1980, p. 118)

What Yalom suggests is that even though we all know we're going to die, we pretend to ourselves that we are not. The reality of the end provokes in us a response that is ubiquitous, and that the response is anxiety. According to Tillich 'Anxiety is the state in which a being is aware of its possible non-being' (1952, p. 44). Anxiety should not be mistaken for fear. Fear, unlike anxiety, has an object, for example, a fear of giving a presentation, or of sharks, and so on. Anxiety, on the other hand, has no object and as such it is often described as 'dread.' It was the Danish philosopher, Søren Kierkegaard, who first carved out this distinction and who is often considered to be the first existentialist. He is famed for saying that, 'Whoever has learned to be anxious in the right way has learned the ultimate' (Kierkegaard, 1844, p. 155). What he tries to convey is that anxiety is a necessary condition of being human in that we are all 'weak' and that we each of us dreads becoming nothingness (death). To combat this existential anxiety or dread, we try to displace it from nothing to something. In this way, if we can shift an unbearable nothing into an unbearable something, then at least we can build some protective architecture around us to fend it off.

This architecture that we erect around ourselves to defend against existential anxiety may come in various guises. Therapists, for example, will encounter clients who cultivate rituals to keep them 'safe' (extreme hand-washing), or take substances (excessive alcohol use), or engage in high-risk behaviour (ongoing unprotected sex) as if through doing so they might cheat death or that death does not apply to them.

According to Heidegger, there are two fundamental modes of existing: inauthentic and authentic. He believed that we have a tendency to fall into a forgetfulness of being in which we exist in a state of mediocrity and 'idle chatter,' focussing on the way things are. In contrast, an authentic mode of existence is one in which we become open to our Being-towards-Death. In other words, we are in awe of the truth of our mortality, or *that* we are. Although we are much of the time lost in inauthenticity, we have the capacity for authenticity. Heidegger says that 'Impassioned freedom towards death is a freedom which has been released from the illusions of the "they" and which is factical, certain of itself, and anxious'(1927, p. 266).

Ultimately, the existential psychotherapist believes that death – or more particularly, one's own death – is the bedrock of all our concerns and when we are attuned to our Being-towards-Death, we can begin to approach life with new vigour, clarity, and direction. Inevitably we fall back into inauthenticity, but this does not necessarily lead to suffering. In fact, to be constantly attuned to one's inevitable death would be an impossible burden. In existential therapy, clients will, like all people, oscillate between authentic and inauthentic modes of being in all moments of their lives. Death is inevitably at the centre of that ongoing process, and perhaps, as Yalom says, it is death that, paradoxically, saves us.

2.2   Do existential therapists work with the unconscious?

An existential psychotherapist is interested in the lived experience of their client's lives. This may well involve an exploration of unconscious phenomena, but not 'the unconscious' as a psychoanalyst might, because the existential therapist does not subscribe to the basis on which 'the' unconscious is predicated, i.e. a Freudian creation to accommodate a dynamic theory of the repression of infantile wishes and powerful pleasure-seeking bodily drives. An existential psychotherapist does not compartmentalise or reduce experience in this way, and instead sees human beings as an ongoing, conscious process that is constantly changing, and crucially has agency that is not at the mercy of unconscious, libidinal conflicts.

To understand what is meant by unconscious for the existentialist, we must first turn to consciousness and intentionality, as from here we shall be better placed to understand how they exist in the theoretical framework. Consciousness is defined by 'intentionality,' which roughly means our *reaching out* or *directedness* into the world, being always conscious *of* something. We are always connected to and participating in the world as sentient beings with both our minds and bodies. Consciousness is an activity in which we are always engaged. For the existentialist, then, this means that there can be no homunculus, or self, that is operating behind a curtain, like the Wizard of Oz. So, for existential psychotherapists, the notion of 'the unconscious' as a chamber of one's secrets that are unknown to oneself is philosophically unsound and unnecessary. Consciousness has neither substance nor structure.

According to the philosopher, Jean-Paul Sartre, if anything about one's consciousness seems unknown, then it is merely hidden in plain sight and we just need to turn our attention to spontaneous experience rather than attribute the notion of the unconscious.

> Spontaneous consciousness is penetrated by a great light without being able to express what this light is illuminating. We are not dealing with an unsolved riddle as the Freudians believe; all is there, luminous... But this 'mystery in broad daylight' is due to the fact that this possession is deprived of the means which would ordinarily permit analysis and conceptualisation. It grasps everything, all at once, without shading, without relief, without connections of grandeur – not that these shades, these values, these reliefs exist somewhere and are hidden from it, but rather because they must be established by another human attitude and because they can exist only by means of and for knowledge.
>
> (Sartre, 1943, pp. 570–571)

For Sartre, consciousness cannot be divided, although he describes two modes of consciousness as being 'pre-reflective' and 'reflective' to show how our intentionality is directed. We relate to our world and environment in a selective way. For example, imagine you are in a busy café talking with a friend over coffee. You may be vaguely aware initially of noise and activity, but as you listen to your friend talking the clatter of cups and conversations around you recede into the background as your attention is focussed on your choice of object (your friend). Your consciousness is not directed towards the other objects in the environment. If however, there is a loud crash your attention would be re-focussed on the impinging clatter. Alternatively, you may overhear some juicy conversation behind you and *almost without actually intending to*, you start to direct your awareness to their conversation and your consciousness becomes more diffuse and has different competing foci as you chose where to direct it.

What, perhaps you are wondering, is the significance of this to therapy? Existential psychotherapists believe we are all in charge of our own future and we are always choosing for ourselves, even when we may tell ourselves we are not. A simple way of describing this is that we are what we do. As we become more aware of our intentionality, it becomes easier to orientate ourselves to the world in ways in which we reflectively choose. The existential therapist will notice what their client is attending to, and what they are not. Rather than motivated by drives from an unconscious, they are driven by an ontological urge to Be. Consciousness, from an existential perspective, is always future-related and embedded in the world.

A client may come for therapy because they believe they are 'trapped' in a relationship or a job. Or they be perplexed about why they keep engaging in high-risk behaviours that could land them in hot water. It is *as though* there is a destiny to these experiences, or rather *as if* the client has been taking important decisions without their own consent! This is how it seems and so can be tempting to believe there are mysterious forces within pushing them along an unwanted path. The existential psychotherapist will listen carefully to how a client is choosing for themselves a course of action over which they tell themselves they have no authorship. A careful investigation must begin into their internal and external world. Unlike the psychoanalyst, the existential therapist does not look *behind*, but *in*, the phenomena presented and will bear in mind that acts inform us of our intentions, even if intention is not always deliberate. The task is to make clear the difference between self-as-agent and self-as-object to allow for a new way of self-reflection.

2.3 What is phenomenology?

The grandfather of pure phenomenology is Edmund Husserl (1836–1938), a mathematician and philosopher, who was very keen to discover an alternative approach to modern science, which he felt was at a point of crisis, putting opinion before the facts. Husserl wanted to grasp the reality around us in an absolute sense. He, and subsequent phenomenologists, is interested by how we comprehend all things in the world, activities, events, entities, and how they present themselves to us. This in many ways is classic metaphysics. How does reality reveal itself to us? What is the difference between how things appear to us and how they really are?

Phenomenology is often described as getting to 'the things themselves.'

If we are to understand phenomenology, we must first comprehend the notion of 'intentionality' which was first conceived by Aristotle, and then returned to us by Husserl's teacher, Franz Brentano, in the nineteenth century (Moran, 2000). Intentionality refers to how human consciousness is projected out into the world towards something. So, there is always an object of our consciousness. We are always conscious *of* something. Husserl notes that '… in perception something is perceived, in imagination something is imagined, in a statement something is stated, in love something is loved, in hate something is hated, in desire something is desired' (1900, p. 554). As you now read the words on this page there is you (subject), the process of perceiving (consciousness), and the object (these words). This whole process is referred to as the intentional arc, and in phenomenology each part is analysed, with a particular method called 'reductions,' in order to reveal the full complexity of reality of the particular situation or moment.

Phenomenology involves paying close attention to the nature of our consciousness. Husserl developed the phenomenological method – a series of reductions – to properly investigate intentional objects. It involves us bracketing our judgements or suspending our natural attitude. The natural attitude is the everyday-ness in which we go about our daily lives in a largely unthinking way that blithely presumes existence. By bracketing our biases we can engage with reality afresh. He referred to this as the Epoche or the 'phenomenological reduction.' From here we can go further with an 'eidetic reduction' to hone in on the essence of the phenomenon in front of us in order to get to its essential qualities, rather than extraneous details. A final 'transcendental reduction' involves us observing the very process by which we are observing, which is a sort of self-observation. This 'transcendental ego' connects to the world as pure consciousness and is the ground for the foundation and constitution of all meaning.

German philosopher, Martin Heidegger (1927), disagreed with Husserl's phenomenology on the basis that it was too abstract. Heidegger was more interested in the distinctions between the 'ontic' and 'ontological,' in other words, facts relating to entities (us) and the nature of Being itself. According to Heidegger, we cannot grasp the world without interpretating it because we ourselves are of the world. We are embedded in the lived world of people, culture, language, objects, activities, and our consciousness and intentionality that make the world meaningful and significant. Although Heidegger was a staunch phenomenologist, for him it is a nonsense to think we can bracket off (as Husserl thought) our way of perceiving the world in order to reach some essence of a phenomenon. Rather than trying to have bird's eye view, we must accept that we are part and parcel of the world, rooted to it and in the thick of it. It is only possible to make our interpretations and meanings of the world from this involved perspective.

How, then, is this relevant to the practice of existential psychotherapy? In practice the existential therapist will adopt a phenomenological attitude to their clients. This involves employing three 'rules.' The first is the rule of Epoche in which we set aside our prejudices and biases about the information and the data the client is bringing, which 'urges us to impose an "openness" on our immediate experience' (Spinelli, 1989, p. 17). The second is the rule of Description in which we describe phenomena rather than explain them. Finally, the third is the rule of Horizontalisation, which pushes us to equalise all aspects of what is being presented so as not to presume or impose a hierarchy on the descriptions.

Through the application of phenomenology, existential therapists remain humble and open to the complexity of experience, perspective, and meanings. The client, like all people, is an ongoing lived process, unique in every way, and always in relationship to the world. The aim is to uncover, very carefully, how the client situates themselves in the world, and what matters to them so that they can see with fresh eyes. Phenomenology is often deceptively simple and very powerful in this way.

2.4   What is the role of the therapist in existential therapy?

The existential psychotherapist is an ordinary, mature person who has grappled, and continues to negotiate, their way through the world of dilemmas and paradoxes that life throws at them. They will have completed a thorough, bona fide, psychotherapy training that will have required them having their own many years of personal psychotherapy in which they endeavour to understand themselves as deeply as possible. An existential psychotherapist will be registered with a body that oversees and regulates their professional practice.

Trust must be earned, and the existential therapist knows this very well. It is for this reason that the relationship one builds with a client is fundamental to the process of the therapy. The therapist will spend much of the time listening intently to the client, gradually building up a picture of the client's internal and external world. More often than not, a person comes for therapy because they are at a crisis point, or because they are feeling vulnerable, lost, or dissatisfied with how things are in their lives. This requires a significant amount of sensitivity from the therapist, who takes the client very seriously, paying particular attention to not just what they are saying, but how they are saying it. For example, a client may be describing the facts of the traumatic way their partner died, but they may be delivering the description in a way that one might read a shopping list. A client may laugh when they explain to the therapist that they were arrested for some dangerous behaviour. The existential psychotherapist does not judge this, but rather remains composed and pays attention to it as a meaningful piece of communication although what that meaning is may not yet be clear and will need unveiling.

In order to gain more understanding for both the therapist and the client, the therapist adopts a phenomenological attitude. In other words, they explore with the client the details of their lives in a descriptive way. There is no explanation offered by the existential therapist, as they remain humble to the process of uncovering the reality of the person's lived experience. They do not make the assumption that because they have had previous clients with similar presenting issues, they understand the true meaning of their current client's concerns. Each person is considered unique.

Boundaries are an essential part of the existential psychotherapist's practice. Having clear parameters of time, money, location, regularity of sessions keeps both the practitioner and the client safe. Consistency in these clear boundaries fosters a sense of trust and reliability in the relationship. The therapist will also be flexible enough to allow for changes, if necessary. The therapeutic relationship involves a constant calibrating of temperature and distance. For example, being too flexible or inconsistent with time and regularity of sessions may result in the client feeling exposed and abandoned. Conversely, rules can be too rigid and result in the client feeling oppressed or restricted. The therapeutic relationship should always be professional, in other words it should stay within the confines of the session. Pursuing a different kind of relationship with a client, such as a business or romantic one, would be considered unethical and must be avoided. Through open dialogue in a professional relationship built on trust, these matters can all be approached and worked with in a way that allows for conducive frame for therapy.

Two of the central tenets of existential psychotherapy are freedom and responsibility. It is with this in mind that the existential psychotherapist will encourage the client to be autonomous and be wary of invitations for them to act on the client's behalf. For this reason, while the therapist is direct, they are seldom directive. The client in existential psychotherapy is learning to be courageous in exploring their own life, which means taking ownership of it, even when it feels scary or overwhelming. The existential psychotherapist is alongside the client in this process. It may be that the therapist will be explicit with the client about their behaviour and choices if, for example, they appear to be acting in bad faith. However, the therapist is not interested in choosing for the client, but rather helping them see how they are always already choosing for themselves.

Some existential psychotherapists may choose to disclose things about themselves, but more often than not the focus remains firmly on the client's experience. This does not mean the encounter is less real or less of a relationship. In fact, the existential therapist does not shy away from any topic, including love and hate even when directed at the therapist themselves. They remain, however, committed to helping the client piece together and clarify their values and assumptions from which their actions and feelings are forged. The existential psychotherapist should be creative, broad-minded, and robust. They do not shy away from difficult conversations. They must be tough enough to be with clients who may have very different, or opposing, values from them. For example, a client may have views and believes that the therapist finds personally abhorrent or even offensive. However, it is not their position to impose their own view, but to remain composed while helping the client to work through the conflicts that their own values create.

2.5 Do existential therapists believe in mental illness?

Language is important because it is how we represent meaning. Like the ideas of people who use it, language changes regularly and this is no less true in the world of psychotherapy. Though there are, historically at least, existential psychotherapists who have written about mental illness or psychopathology of the individual, they tend to have often been psychiatrists who were working in clinical settings in a time when psychoanalysis was still the prevailing paradigm and language relating to 'treatment' of 'patients' was still relevant. European psychiatrists in the twentieth century, such as Karl Jaspers (1883–1969), tried to move away from what they saw as the limitations of applying positivist methods of science to the mind, and so strived to replace definitions of mental illness with a description and study of experience (Cooper et al., 2019).

Since then, there has been ever-stronger motivation towards a careful description and exploration of the whole person and their lived experience of their existence. Deurzen notes, however, that it is still the case that 'The churches of psychotherapy have become oppressive forces that mould personalities and that confuse pathology with the struggle to survive' (1997, p. 2).

Existential psychotherapists work in many different settings across the world, from private practice to hospital clinics and so are obliged, and wise, to make themselves familiar with the various terminologies used by different sections of our society, including the world of medicine and psychiatry. What is different, however, is how we choose to conceptualise phenomena presented to us by people under our professional therapeutic care.

This difference is revealed in the work of Yalom, who charts how pathology comes from anxiety in an individual's struggles with what he describes as the four main ultimate concerns of existence, namely death, freedom, isolation, and meaninglessness.

> ...psychopathology is a graceless inefficient mode of coping with anxiety. An existential paradigm assumes that anxiety emanates from the individual's confrontation with the ultimate concerns in existence.
>
> (Yalom, 1980, p. 110)

The way in which a person navigates through these ultimate concerns will indicate their level of distress or disturbance. An example Yalom gives is that of the schizophrenic patient whose sense of omnipotence can be viewed as armoured defence against death. Similarly, in a more pedestrian example, the 'workaholic' defends against the reality that there will be a point when they no longer 'advance' in their projects and time gets the better of them in the form of their inevitable demise. Theologian Paul Tillich echoes this in his statement that 'neurosis is the way of avoiding non-being by avoiding being' (1952, p. 66).

Although, as you can see, there are words that hark back to the language of pathology and mental illness, many existential psychotherapists prefer to see people as having problems in living rather than being 'ill' as such. Perhaps the most vehement of them is psychiatrist Thomas Szasz (1920–2012) who denied there was such a thing as mental illness at all, referring to it as a myth (Szasz, 1961).

All people struggle with the givens of existence and the dilemmas they throw up. The existential psychotherapist will have people referring themselves for therapy who have either been diagnosed with one thing or another such as anxiety, depression, or a personality disorder. Often people self-diagnose because they confuse pathology with a struggle to survive. In therapy, what is aimed for is not the alleviation of symptoms (although this may well happen), but the development of understanding about one's predicaments in life and living, and crucially, one's own part in it.

The existential psychotherapist will take very seriously a person's experience, including if this relates to labels they may use about themselves to describe a mental illness. Rather than buying into the language which can obfuscate the truth, the therapist will enquire and explore the client's experience of what it means for them to struggle with, for example, an anxiety disorder. Through the use of careful phenomenological method (described elsewhere in this part), the therapist and the client together will tease out what is at the heart of the matter, whether that is a fantasy or wish to avoid death, or a denial of their freedom, and so on.

It is worth mentioning the role of anxiety here. The client who is labouring under extreme anxiety or panic attacks must learn to listen to their anxiety rather than run from it or try to extinguish. Existential psychotherapists take the view that anxiety is essential as a felt response to the elemental paradoxes of life. Once the anxious client starts to confront their inauthenticity and bad faith, they can begin to harness anxiety in a way that liberates and propels them forward. According to Sartre (1943), we are 'condemned to be free,' which means we are responsible for living authentically and creating ourselves afresh. This of course takes courage, and the existential psychotherapist is often the midwife of this courage in their work with clients. Once this begins to happen, the need for labels of mental illness becomes redundant as the client is open to facing facticity and the socio-cultural world to which they belong and can then make a worthwhile life-project from within the limits of their situation.

2.6   What is a mind and how is it seen through an existential lens?

Perhaps everyone thinks they have one, but who can say what 'the' mind or 'a' mind really is? There has been much debate, over millennia, about it and views today tend to be split between those who think the mind cannot simply be reduced to the chemical and neurological and those who think it can.

There are many different definitions of mind, too numerous to include here.

Crudely, we might describe a mind as a complex process of mental phenomena or the experience of consciousness. Naturally, and perhaps logically, when we think of consciousness we tend to conceive of a 'self' that is conscious, and this leads us to ask for further definitions.

To give some context, it is the philosopher Rene Descartes (1596–1650) who is both credited and criticised with introducing what is considered a 'dualism' in philosophy and science, i.e. a clear distinction between the mind and the body. This is often referred to as the 'Cartesian split.' Descartes' position was to start by doubting everything because he thought that we cannot trust anything, including our senses, as they are often deceptive and unreliable in delivering the truth. The one thing he thought he could trust was, ironically, his doubt. The very fact that he was thinking and doubting was one thing that was not a deception and this gave rise to his famous dictum, *cogito ergo sum*, which translates as 'I think, therefore I am.' This dualism made a long-lasting mark on philosophy and science, and it was only really until the work of philosopher and mathematician Edmund Husserl (1859–1938) that the Cartesian split was bridged. Husserl developed a method of understanding the world by uniting all acts of consciousness, both of the subject and of the object. This method is known as 'phenomenology' and is described elsewhere in this part.

From a phenomenological and existential perspective, we cannot conceive of the mind without including the body.

Heidegger (1927) used the term '*Dasein*' (being-in-the-world) to refer to human beings because this use of language brings into focus the merged relationship between the consciousness and the world. For philosopher Maurice Merleau-Ponty to understand the relationship between the mind and the body, we have to turn our attention to the problems of perception and embodiment. All mental life is embodied and as such, 'knowledge is in the hands' (Merleau-Ponty, 1945, p. 143). The body and the mind as a co-existing unity is important to the existential psychotherapist because they are both the conduit and the projector of all experience. Together the mind and the body form, arguably, what for most people is experienced as one's 'self.'

According to existential psychotherapist Orah Krug,

> The meanings an individual makes from lived experiences create a set of self and world constructs, essentially a set of beliefs regarding self, others, and the world. These constructs are understood as an individual's personal world and context that varies, continually influenced by the cultural, historical, and cosmological experiences of each individual.
>
> (Krug, 2019, p. 259)

The personal world is, in existential psychotherapy, considered the innermost realm of selfhood. It is here that we identify ourselves as 'me' and as separate and distinct from the realms of 'not me.' The self is, like consciousness, a perpetual movement and its formation 'is not a task of childhood only, it is a constant challenge and is undertaken at every minute and hour of the day' (Deurzen, 1997, p. 121).

For Sartre, consciousness is grounded in the body, is future-directed, and not defined by the past. It is one's sense of becoming which is a fundamental human reality and this self is always connected to, and co-created by, the world in what he describes as a 'circuit of selfness.' At the heart of consciousness is a lack. Unlike a psychoanalytical view of the self as based on pleasure-seeking drives, Sartre's consciousness is ontological in that it is a desire of Being. He said that 'man is the being whose project it is to be God' (Sartre, 1943, p. 566), by which he meant that consciousness is a 'lacking' because it can never be a substantial self on account of it being a constantly moving project.

How does any of this relate to the practice of psychotherapy? We might think of the mind and self as something we identify as 'me' and this 'me' is in time, and in a state of flux. 'I' am being acted upon by the world and acting upon it at all times, even when I think I am doing nothing. When a person comes for therapy they may have what Merleau-Ponty (ibid.) referred to as a 'sedimented' view of themselves. They define themselves as a depressed person or an unlovable person, for example, and act like this is a fixed truth about them. For an existential psychotherapist, as we live in time we cannot help but change, and so we can project a future that frees us from the sedimented past. In a more pedestrian way, people often become trapped in an identity they give themselves, which is then confirmed by society, such as 'lawyer,' 'waiter,' 'doctor,' or 'husband.' When a person behaves as though they *are* those things, they are considered to be acting inauthentically by denying the reality of their freedom. Bringing into focus the nature of one's self and inauthenticity makes for fertile ground from which can be cultivated a more authentic way of being oneself, which can never really be defined.

2.7 What is Socratic dialogue and how do existential psychotherapists use Socratic dialogue therapeutically?

It is difficult to convey just how significant Socrates is to Western philosophy given that his influence seems to have reached into almost every realm of its origins. As Nehamas puts it, 'with the exception of the Epicureans, every philosophical school in antiquity, whatever its orientation, saw in him either its actual founder or the type of person to whom its adherents were to aspire' (1999, p. 99).

So, who was he and why was, and is, he so significant? Socrates (469–399 BCE) was a man of ancient Athens, who, despite his pervasive presence in philosophy, wrote down absolutely nothing in his lifetime. Everything we have come to know of him is second hand, passed down to us by other great thinkers such as Plato. By all accounts, Socrates was someone who made people think, introducing doubt where there was apparent certainty. He would engage in conversation with anyone and on any topic and often frustrated and enthralled people in equal measure.

Socrates believed that in a similar way as a midwife helps a woman deliver her baby, an interlocutor asking the right questions can draw out from a person wisdom and knowledge that already exists within them. In arguments, Socrates sought definitions from his debaters but was never himself satisfied with his own grasp on whatever it was under discussion. He considered himself to be ignorant and emphasised that our sense of our certainty about matters should be approached most critically. As Deurzen and Kenward note, the Socratic method has 'a paradoxical character, for it is a way of eliciting what a person is unaware that he knows, or of demonstrating that he does not know what he thinks he knows.' (2005, p. 189). At the same time, Socrates believed, famously, that 'the unexamined life is not worth living.'

Despite being almost universally revered, Socrates was so adept at turning accepted truths on their head, that in the end, he was deemed by Greek authorities to be too subversive to the Athenian culture of the time and was sentenced to death.

Socratic dialogue, broadly then, is a process of dialogue based on questioning that inspires critical thinking and analysis.

In iterative process, the aim is to find knowledge, understanding, and truth. Given the emotional and sensitive nature of psychotherapy practice, the process of Socratic dialogue should perhaps be employed judiciously and empathically to help to structure dialogue that does not descend into combative argument.

Therapists know that emotional biases are resistant to logical argument as 'in the storms of emotionality, a person might feel a desperate need to cling onto irrational certainties' (Wharne, 2021). That is why when a client says something like 'I'm a loser,' it is unhelpful and unwise to offer ostensibly reassuring platitudes such as 'Of course you're not.' Instead, however, a therapist might, if the time is right, begin to use Socratic questioning to enquire further into that person's experience.

Consider the following example. Samir comes for therapy because he feels very down on himself, thinking of himself as one of life's losers. His relationship recently ended. His partner left him for someone else, a woman, with whom she'd been having an affair for some time. Samir blames himself, believing that if he had worked less his wife would never have left him.

No two existential psychotherapists are the same and so inevitably will not approach the same person in the same manner, but for the purposes of demonstration, perhaps a therapist could approach Samir's difficulty using the following steps:

1 Listen carefully and empathically to what he says, the bases on which he is making the claim 'I'm a loser.'
2 Reflect back to him what he has said, summarising what you have heard. Ask Samir to clarify his position or view and then repeat it back to him. For example, 'Your wife left you for someone else and you believe this was your fault because you were inattentive as a husband, and you think you are a loser.'

3 Clarify definitions and refine. Ask Samir to explain what they mean by the word 'loser.' Open this out. What evidence to the contrary might there be? Have there ever been times when Samir was not a loser?
4 Encourage Samir to discover facts, beliefs, and assumptions that underpin his position and to move from the specific to the global and widen the context: Does Samir's idea that he is a loser apply in all contexts/situations? You might ask 'Would you say that all people whose relationships end are losers?' or 'Other than one partner working too much, are there any other possible reasons why relationships end?'
5 Restate and reformulate Samir's position so that he can come to see any flaws in his thinking and begin to question his own reasoning. The Socratic approach is not to give answers, but to ask questions and reclarifying.

You can see that although Socrates was no therapist, his analytic, questioning, style affords us a way to challenge our perceptions, beliefs, and concomitant feelings about ourselves and the world. Existential therapists, like any therapist, may or may not choose to employ this form of questioning in their practice, as much of how we operate will be dependent on the unique context that every client brings. Socrates can however, like Apollo himself, be a beacon of light to an otherwise clouded situation.

2.8 What is the framework of existential psychotherapy?

Unlike so many other approaches, there is no founding father of existential psychotherapy, which has instead been developed and distilled through philosophy across the ages. Existential psychotherapists are, at heart, philosophers who lean on the vast richness of Western philosophy going as far back, if not further, than Heraclitus (540–480 BC), who was famous for instructing us to confront the impermanence of everything. Many existential psychotherapists may well also draw on Eastern philosophy for inspiration. However, more specifically, it is existential philosophy on which our approach is based.

> Existential philosophy focuses on human existence – a word derived from the Latin *existere* meaning 'to stand out' – and existential therapists often use the phenomenological method which provides existential thought with a practical way of investigating the world.
>
> (du Plock & Tantam, 2019, p. 133)

The method of phenomenology referred to in the above quote is described elsewhere in this part. Briefly, the aim is to describe experience rather than explain it. It should be said that many people believe that the uniqueness of existential psychotherapy is in its resistance to being defined and systematised. Indeed, one of the earlier American existential therapists, Rollo May, noted that existential psychology,

> …does not purport to found a new school as over and against the other schools or to give a new technique of therapy as over against other techniques. It seeks rather, to analyse the structure of human existence – an enterprise which, if successful, should yield an understanding of the reality underlying all situations of human beings in crisis.
>
> (May, 1958, p. 7)

There are four different schools of existential psychotherapy, adumbrated elsewhere in this part of the book. Each embraces clinical work in its own way. For example, the existential-humanistic school has now developed an integrative arm, the purpose of which is to 'maximise freedom' against various restrictive and expansive 'dreads' faced by all humans (Schneider, 2008). For the purposes of this book, which is limited in scope, we shall be focusing on the framework of existential-phenomenological school.

We should perhaps start with the assumptions inherent in this existential approach to psychotherapy. After all, every modality of therapy has its own set of assumptions that underpin the philosophy from which it operates and conceptualises phenomena. Existential psychotherapy holds arguably at least three basic assumptions:

1 Sense of life can be made. Rather than given to us, meaning and order in life is created by each of us.
2 Even though we do not choose the life we are given or what it throws at us, we always have the responsibility and choice about how we respond to it.
3 There are universal limitations and boundaries that govern the world such as gravity, time, pain, the existence of others, and the weather, to name but a few (Deurzen, 2002).

Existential therapy is fundamentally an ontological, rather than purely psychological, endeavour and as such we do not categorise people in terms of personality or character traits. Instead, we seek to chart an individual's existence as broadly and deeply as possible. While there is no rule or prescribed way of doing that, there has developed over time a map that delineates four realms of existence (Binswanger, 1963; Yalom, 1980; Deurzen-Smith, 1997), which has become known as the 'four worlds' model. These worlds are physical, social, personal, and spiritual, and often (because of their conceptual heritage) go by their respective German names, i.e. *Umwelt, Mitwelt, Eigenwelt*, and *Uberwelt*. An existential psychotherapist can use this four-world map to get a sense of how their client is living with the paradoxes and tensions inherent in life and at each level.

The *Umwelt/Physical* world concerns our physical environment, the natural world around us, our body and health, and material things. The tensions here lie between life and death, health and illness, wealth and poverty, and pleasure and pain.

Next, the *Mitwelt/Social* world concerns the way we relate to others and the tensions here lie in negotiating between belonging and isolation, acceptance and rejection, love and hate, and admiration and condemnation.

Third, the *Eigenwelt/Personal* world concerns the relationship which we have with ourselves. It is our inner world and sense of 'selfhood.' The tensions in this realm are around integrity and disintegration, identity and confusion, perfection and imperfection, and confidence and doubt.

Lastly, the *Uberwelt/Spiritual* world concerns our relationship to ideas, values, meaning, and the unknown. Tensions in this dimension can be considered to be between meaning and meaninglessness, serenity and guilt, purpose and futility, and good and evil.

This framework of existential psychotherapy allows for a full exploration of each dimension. At all times there is, to greater or lesser degrees, anxiety and this must be embraced and understood rather than ignored or negated.

2.9   Why have different schools emerged and what are the main differences?

There are considered to be four main different schools, or branches, of the existential approach to psychotherapy: daseinsanalysis, existential-phenomenological (once referred to as the British school), existential-humanistic and integrative, and logotherapy (Deurzen, 2019).

Daseinsanalysis was, arguably, the first on the stage and was developed, largely, by two European psychiatrists and psychoanalysts, Ludwig Binswanger and Merdard Boss. At the time, during the early 1940s, it was the 'first systematic approach to existential psychotherapy' (Craig, 2019). At this particular point in time, many European psychiatrists and psychoanalysts were becoming disillusioned with Freud's rather mechanical model of the mind. They believed it fell considerably short of reaching an understanding of the whole person. Binswanger and Boss were both immersed in continental philosophy, especially the work of Martin Heidegger (1888–1976) and they used their understanding of his work to develop a new way of conceptualising the human being which would re-shape reductionist, Freudian psychotherapy into an ontological endeavour. In other words, less focussed on basic drives as the basis of human behaviour, and more attending to a person's lived experience of existence, to Being itself.

The defining feature of Daseinsanalysis is to be found in the name. Heidegger referred to the human being as '*Dasein*,' which is a German word often translated as '*being-in-the-world*,' or '*there-being*.' He used this word to emphasise the specialness of human being as an entity that is inextricably connected to the world. Daseinsanalysis is fundamentally a philosophical enterprise and approach to the individual. It is, at its core, phenomenological and is concerned with the shared constitutional characteristics of *Dasein*. There is no place for psychopathology as all phenomena are real in their own way and must be treated equally.

Although once referred to as the 'British school of existential psychotherapy' it is now more commonly referred to as 'existential-phenomenological' therapy to account for both the diversity of its contributors over the years and its global reach. Main protagonists include Emmy van Deurzen, Ernesto Spinelli, and Hans Cohn.

In Britain, back in the 1970s, the psychiatrist Ronald Laing (1927–1989) and others highlighted the existential and ontological aspects to human suffering, and they promulgated the 'anti-psychiatry' movement which railed against the medical orthodoxy of the time. What was lacking, however, was a coherent, disciplined application of existential philosophy to psychotherapy and in response to this lacking, in 1988, psychologist Emmy van Deurzen established the Society for Existential Analysis in London. Dutch-born Deurzen had studied philosophy before training as a clinical psychologist in France. She worked alongside Laing for a time in the 1970s before becoming disillusioned by his 'flawed' practices (Deurzen, 1997). With the establishment of the Society of Existential Analysis and various training institutes with online training programmes, existential-phenomenological psychotherapy has proliferated. Unlike the other 'schools,' this one is deeply rooted in the discipline of philosophy, drawing on the classical principles of debate and dialogue. The aim of existential-phenomenology is to help the client 'meticulously examine' their life in pursuit of wisdom, which is done by '… investigating all that is and can be known, with great vigor and determination' (Deurzen, 2019, p. 128).

Across the pond in the United States in the 1950s, psychology had been dominated by two schools, behaviourism and Freudian psychoanalysis. However, there was growing unrest and dissatisfaction among the intellectuals of these groups about the limitations of these deterministic schools, specifically the lack of focus on the existential, human capacities and qualities that make a person such as their choices and values (Yalom, 1980).

What emerged from this was 'humanistic psychology,' the major proponents of which were Carl Rogers, Rollo May, Abraham Maslow, and James Bugental, among others. This new wave of psychology was espoused as the existential antidote to the reductionist past of psychology, but became rather diluted and diffuse due to its inclusivity to all-and-sundry. Deriving from this, more recently, is the 'existential-humanistic' school. Current proponents of this include Americans such as Irvin Yalom and Kirk Schneider. The school differs from the more continental schools of Daseinsanalysis or the existential-phenomenological school, in that it is more pragmatic and places more emphasis on the here-and-now experiential, and the striving for the full realisation of human potential. According to Schneider (2019), the aim of existential-humanistic (EH) therapy is to 'set clients free' by discovering meaning and awe. He notes that the approach is

> Facilitated ... via whole-bodied presence – or the holding and illuminating of that which is palpably significant between therapist and client and within the client. Akin to a mirror, presence helps guide the EH therapist ... toward two ... questions: 'How is the client presently living?' and 'How is the client willing to live?' at every point of the encounter.
>
> (ibid., p. 231)

Although its main, current, proponent is the Austrian psychiatrist, Alfred Längle, the fourth school, 'logotherapy,' came into being through Viktor Frankl (1905–1997) who, like many in his day, had grown sceptical of the reductionism inherent in Freudian psychology. Most notably, perhaps, Frankl developed his principles while struggling to find meaning in life as a prisoner in a Nazi concentration camp. '*Logos*' is Greek for 'meaning.' Frankl believed we needed to consider human beings as 'whole' rather than as parts, and that our main concern is with finding meaning in each situation. Unlike in other existential approaches, Frankl was often directive and developed techniques such as 'paradoxical intention' for dealing with anxiety-laden dilemmas. Perhaps not surprisingly given his background, Frankl believed that life always involves pain, guilt, and death, but that it is from here, from our suffering, that we develop meaning and purpose.

2.10 How can philosophy help with emotional and psychological problems?

As soon as a person begins to question something such as 'why do we die?' or 'what is the right way to live?' they employ philosophy. Perhaps the earliest philosophical systems developed as early as 4000 BC as depicted in the hieroglyphs of the ancient Egyptians in relation to the afterlife. However, the word philosophy comes from the Greek *philo* (love) and *sophia* (wisdom), literally meaning 'love of wisdom' and has spawned today what we refer to as Western philosophy.

In the writings of ancient Greek and Roman philosophers, we can see proposed systems aimed and either understanding the nature of reality or proposing the best way to live, through reflection and wisdom. As early as Heraclitus (540–480 BC) there was advice about how to cope with change. For Heraclitus, life is an ongoing process of which we are an integral part. Everything is in constant flux and so we should embrace change rather than resist it. Through Socrates (470–399 BC) we learn to be sceptical and questioning of what appears to be truth and thereby remain humble in the pursuit of it. Later, the Roman Stoics Seneca, Epictetus, and Marcus Aurelius entreat us to be rational, self-disciplined, and heroic. They show us how to manage our expectations and to live in harmony with nature (Howard, 2000). There are those, for example, who live life unquestioningly, and it is not until they hit upon something that challenges them to reflect, such as their own ill-health or inevitable death, that the cracks in their approach to living begin to show. These ancient philosophers are as relevant today as they were then.

Indeed, what can be more profound than taking stock of who you are, what you believe, and how you live in all dimensions of existence? This is active, lived, philosophy, and it is what the existential psychotherapist encourages in their work with their clients. Three well-known existential philosophers, Nietzsche, Heidegger, and Sartre, have afforded us new ways to approach the human condition.

You will read, in more detail, about all three of these existential philosophers elsewhere in this book. In summary, Nietzsche (1883) teaches us to be passionate and courageous masters of our own destiny and to transcend what we have held to be our 'selves.' Heidegger (1927) brings us to an awareness of authenticity and inauthenticity by recognising our enmeshment with the world, others, and our own inevitable death. For Sartre (1943), a person is not defined by the past, but rather future-oriented, irrefutably free, and responsible. So, let us see how philosophy can be applied in the practice of psychotherapy.

Everything you say and do reveals to the world something about the values and beliefs you hold, whether that is how you treat others, view yourself, or live your life. It is only through careful analysis of your values that you can really begin to choose authentically for yourself because you become aware of those beliefs that are implicit. For example, a client may tell their therapist that they are fed up and furious about being walked all over by people in their life, and that while they do so much for everybody else, they do not get afforded the same respect.

The explicit issue is that the client feels they deserve respect that they are not getting from others in their life who they feel they are respecting. Socrates, however, would want us to clarify for this client what their idea of 'respect' was and on what basis they believed they deserved it. Marcus Aurelius might help this client to reassess and recalibrate their expectations, and that there appears to be an assumption that others in the client's life must have the same ideas and values of 'respect' as them. Nietzsche would nudge us to wonder why this client continued to act in ways that gave rise to resentment and why they placed so much emphasis on the opinions of others. Through a Heideggerian lens, we would want to know what the client's actions aimed at. What do they set out to achieve by making themselves available to others in a way that is never reciprocated, but is resented? Sartre would tell us that this client is living in bad faith and that they are not being responsible for themselves and instead prefer to tell themselves they are stuck in a certain mode of being with others over which they have no choice.

From the example above you can begin to see how the existential psychotherapist uses philosophy not as a prescription but as a map on which they can chart the way in which their clients make meaning from their engagement with, or disengagement from, their choices, freedom, and responsibility. Therapy is an art cultivated over many years and must be practiced sensitively and judiciously. Although the existential psychotherapist will make philosophical formulations in their minds, they do not talk about philosophy with the client. The language must be ordinary and relevant to the person's predicament in a way that can help them rather than make them defensive or confused.

Once a client begins to employ a philosophical attitude to their life they often discover they have more room, internally, to manoeuvre. They develop a more constructively critical inner voice that can guide them through the complexities of challenges of daily living.

Further reading

Bakewell, S. (2017). *At the Existential Café: Freedom, Being & Apricot Cocktails*. Penguin-Random House.

Deurzen, E. van, & Arnold-Baker, C. (2018). *Existential Therapy: Distinctive Features*. Routledge.

Warnock, M. (1970). *Existentialism*. OPUS.

References

Binswanger, L. (1963). *Being-in-the-World* (J. Needleman, trans.). Basic Books.

Cooper, M., Craig, E., & Deurzen, van E. (2019). Introduction: What is existential therapy? In E. van Deurzen, E. Craig, A. Längle, K. Schneider, D. Tantam, & S. du Plock (Eds.), *The Wiley World Handbook of Existential Psychotherapy*. Wiley & Sons, 1–27.

Craig, E. (2019). The history of daseinsanalysis. In E. van Deurzen, E. Craig, A. Längle, K. Schneider, D. Tantam, & S. du Plock (Eds.), *The Wiley World Handbook of Existential Therapy*. Wiley & Sons, 33–54.

Deurzen, E. van (2002). *Existential Counselling & Psychotherapy in Practice* (2nd ed.). Sage.

Deurzen, E. van (2019). Existential-phenomenological therapy. In E. van Deurzen, E. Craig, A. Längle, K. Schneider, D. Tantam, & S. du Plock (Eds.), *The Wiley World Handbook of Existential Therapy*. Wiley & Sons, 127–131.

Deurzen, E. van, & Kenward, R. (2005). *Dictionary of Existential Psychotherapy & Counselling*. Sage.

Deurzen-Smith, E. van (1997). *Everyday Mysteries: Existential Dimensions of Psychotherapy*. Routledge.

du Plock, S., & Tantam, D. (2019). History of existential-phenomenological therapy. In E. van Deurzen, E. Craig, A. Längle, K. Schneider, D. Tantam, & S. du Plock (Eds.), *The Wiley World Handbook of Existential Therapy*. Wiley & Sons, 33–44.

Heidegger, M. (1927). *Being and Time* (J. Macquarrie & E.S. Robinson, trans.). Harper and Row (1962).

Howard, A. (2000). *Philosophy for Counselling & Psychotherapy – Pythagoras to Postmodernism*. Palgrave.

Husserl, E. (1900). *Logical Investigations* (J.N. Findlay, trans.). Routledge (1970).

Kierkegaard, S. (1844). *The Concept of Anxiety* (R. Thomte, trans.). Princeton University Press (1980).

May, R. (1958). The origins and significance of the existential movement in psychology. In R. May, E. Angel, & H. Ellenberger (Eds.), *Existence: A New Dimension in Psychiatry and Psychology*. Basic Books, 3–36.

Merleau-Ponty, M. (1945). *Phenomenology of Perception* (C. Smith, trans.). Routledge (1962).

Moran, D. (2000). *Introduction to Phenomenology*. Routledge.

Nehamas, A. (1999). *Virtues of Authenticity*. Princeton University Press.

Nietzsche, F. (1883). *Thus Spoke Zarathustra* (R. J. Hollingdale, trans.). Penguin (1961).

Sartre, J-P. (1943). *Being and Nothingness – An Essay on Phenomenological Ontology* (H. Barnes, trans.). Philosophical Library (1956).

Schneider, K. (2008). *Existential-Integrative Psychotherapy, Guideposts to the Core of Practice*. Routledge.

Schneider, K. (2019). Existential-Humanistic and Existential-Integrative Therapy. In E. van Deurzen, E. Craig, A. Längle, K. Schneider, D. Tantam, & S. du Plock (Eds.), *The Wiley World Handbook of Existential Therapy*. Wiley & Sons, 231–233.

Spinelli, E. (1989). *Demystifying Therapy*. Constable.

Szasz, T. (1961). *The Myth of Mental Illness*. Harper.

Tillich, P. (1952). *The Courage to Be*. Yale University Press.

Wharne, S. (2021). Socratic questioning and irony in psychotherapeutic practices. *Journal of Contemporary Psychotherapy*. https://doi.org/10.1007/s10879-021-09514-7

Yalom, I. (1980). *Existential Psychotherapy*. Basic Books.

Part 3

Existential skills and practice

Questions about the way existential therapists work

Jo Molle

3.1 Are existential therapists free to work in any way they want?

Existential therapy can be summarised as being a philosophical rather than psychological approach, concerned with understanding how people live rather than the explanation and eradication of specific problems. Rather than distress being the result of an individual's pathology, distress is seen as evidence of problems in living. Through the development of a 'real' relationship (Cohn, 1997) an existential therapist will, with the client, explore, clarify, and elucidate the difficulties and dilemmas of the human condition.

Existential philosophy emphasises openness, suspension of certainty, and suspicion of over-simplification, and 'it is difficult not to conclude that there are as many unique expressions of existential therapy as there are unique beings who engage and practise it' (Spinelli, 2014, p. 12). Adams and Deurzen (2016) note that there are no absolute rules or regulations in existential therapy; prescribed techniques prohibit therapists from a full understanding of how clients live, experience, and think about their lives. And so, unlike practitioners from other approaches, existential therapists have remained relatively reserved in describing ways of working (Adams, 2013). This poses a particular challenge for this part of this book; how might we describe how existential therapists work if there are no commonly accepted techniques?

DOI: 10.4324/9781003355700-4

Existential therapists as in most other therapeutic approaches are responsible for developing a personal style founded on principles. While existential therapists might include compatible techniques from other approaches, these are integrated in a disciplined way. It is important to note here, that while an existential therapist may integrate compatible techniques, using the body in a therapeutic way such as those in mindfulness-based practices, they tend not to be the focus of existential therapy. Instead, the focus is on exploring the experience of the client in a phenomenological way. However, some practitioners have incorporated the body into their clinical work by practicing a skill called focusing. For more information, the reader is directed to the work of Eugene Gendlin, a philosopher and psychotherapist.

Existential therapy, therefore, is not an anything-that-goes model but an approach that is based on the key principles of existential philosophy and phenomenology already outlined in the previous parts. Fundamentally an existential practitioner will adopt a phenomenological attitude and will listen with an openness to all possibilities and different worldviews.

The phenomenological attitude in practice

As Cohn (1997) highlights, phenomenology aims to describe experience in a way that is uncontaminated by foreknowledge, bias, and explanation. Husserl first devised phenomenology to be a disciplined systematic method for exploring events and things. He described three attitudes (Husserl termed these reductions) designed to enable questioning of usual assumptions made about the world so that he could arrive at the essence of an experience (see Part 2). These can be summarised as follows:

1 Phenomenological reduction (or Epoché): the suspension of judgement where prejudice and points of view are noted and set aside.

2 Eidetic reduction: where all possible aspects of the phenomena are noted so that the essential qualities can be determined.
3 Transcendental reduction: where there is a shift from thinking to reflection and the senses or meanings phenomena have for us are explored.

Existential therapists have greatly benefitted from the application of these reductions to practice. Though, it should be noted that there are differences between Husserl's phenomenological attitude and the application of the phenomenological attitude in existential therapy. Husserl (1900) aimed for his method to arrive at the 'essence' of the experience itself; existential therapists however, with the emphasis on Sartre's proposition that 'existence proceeds essence,' are less interested in essence and are more interested in existence. Nonetheless, by adopting a phenomenological attitude we can help clients (and ourselves) gain a deeper understanding of the assumptions made about the world and how responses are shaped by these assumptions. By staying with and attuning to the lifeworld of the client through dialogue, the existential therapist can begin to challenge the client's expectations of others, and perceptions of how others expect the client to be (Spinelli, 2006). As Adams and Deurzen (2016, p. 40) state:
    'In following the rules of phenomenology:

*   I form a clearer conception of how I relate to the world.
*   I come to understand the world better.
*   I understand the self which is created in the process of relating.'

Ultimately being aware of how we make sense of the world leads to a more open, honest, and clear understanding of the challenges in living, and enables a more purposeful and active way of being.

The aims of existential therapy

Broadly, existential therapy aims to enable a confrontation with essential aspects of life, so that a client can move towards living a more 'authentic' and free existence. May stated that 'the purpose of psychotherapy is to set people free... I believe that the therapist's function should be to help people become free to be aware of and to experience their possibilities' (1981, pp. 19–20). Yalom describes two aspects of this process. The first is to 'encourage the individual to look within... to attend [and to accept] his or her existential situation' (Yalom, 1980, p. 14). This exploration enables a confrontation with the ultimate concerns of existence, outlined by Yalom as death, isolation, meaninglessness, and freedom. This confrontation 'is painful but ultimately healing' (ibid., p. 14). Once challenges in living have been explored and there is sufficient acceptance of responsibility, the therapist embarks on an effort alongside the client 'to transform a sense of personal dissatisfaction into a decision to change and then into the act of change' (ibid., p. 73). Confronting and challenging clients is the focus of the next Part.

3.2 Do existential therapists confront, ask questions, and challenge more than other therapists?

This is a difficult question to produce an absolute answer to as each therapist will practice in their own unique style. However, as existential therapy is based on a philosophical approach, questioning and challenging are essential parts of the process. It is, as Adams and Deurzen state, 'the heart of existential therapy' (2016, p. 41). When we take a curious and questioning attitude to our experience, we are more able to look behind the structures that we impose on our thinking and gain insight into how we live.

Questioning in existential therapy is conducted in a spirit of curiosity and not criticism and, to enable a client to think through their reactions. Deurzen emphasises this by stating that 'The client is encouraged not to take anything for granted, but to question, clarify, explain, define and explore, not for the benefit of the counsellor or therapist, but to learn to reflect' (2012, p. 114). Socratic dialogue is one way in which we can seek knowledge, understanding, and truth (see Section 2.7). However, existential practitioners use a wide variety of skills to elucidate and challenge.

Adams (2013) describes the core skills of existential practice as consisting of two parts (epoché and verification) that are sustained by attention and bridged by horizontalisation. Each of these aspects is described below.

Attention

The ability to attend to a client is a cornerstone in most therapies. We attend to our clients with openness and care while also attending to ourselves, so that we do not unduly influence the client.

Epoché

However, it is important to note that we will always influence the client in ways that are beyond our awareness, and it is while we are attending to the client, that we become aware of our biases and assumptions that need to be bracketed (put aside) and reflected upon. Bracketing during the session is not simply the removal of arising assumptions and biases, but rather actively noting how and when they may influence the work.

Epoché is a word to describe a whole process, from attending to the client, eliciting descriptions, noticing our own biases, assumptions, and judgements, and then bracketing them to return to attending to the client. There are two further aspects of this process: description and equalisation.

Description

Existential therapists will utilise clarification 'what' and 'how' questions rather than explore the 'why.' For example, questions like how do you mean?, what's that like?, can you say more? aim to elicit detailed descriptions rather than explanations.

Equalisation

Every aspect of the client's communication should be given equal significance unless the client has indicated otherwise. The things of importance will emerge by themselves if the client is allowed to shape the landscape.

Horizontalisation

This can be seen as a bridge between the attending and clarifying skills used at the beginning of existential therapy and those employed a little later to interpret and challenge. Horizontalisation involves the understanding of the client's experience from their perspective or the horizon of their own worldview; this will include exploring familial, social, political, and cultural pressures (Deurzen & Arnold-Baker, 2018).

As Adams writes:

> Understanding the context of our experiences is vital and the client needs to find a way, facilitated by us, to stand back from their immediate issues and see them in the context of their whole life – past, present, and future.
>
> (Adams, 2019, p. 171)

Verification

Verification's aim is to make links and explore what may be hidden meanings, common factors, and recurring themes and to challenge them in the spirit of creative uncertainty. Clients may be asked questions such as:

- What is your part in this?
- Is this a familiar feeling?
- On the one hand, you may feel X but on the other, you feel Y.

Questioning here is designed to open discussion rather than close it; and while there is a more hermeneutic interpretive function, we discipline ourselves to compare the sense we make of the experience to what is actually presented by the client. We will explore this further in Section 3.4.

Joy and humour in therapy

Therapy is a serious practice; and often the focus is on fear, anguish, and sorrow as well as aspects of the human condition such as meaninglessness, isolation, and death. However, the practice of therapy involves the formation of a relationship between two human beings, and in that encounter, joy and humour can also be present, as they are in all other relationships. Joy can be defined as a feeling of great pleasure and happiness and indicates an ownership of what is valued (Gibson & Tantam, 2017). In existential therapy, all emotions are important and are explored; all emotions are meaningful as they indicate something about choices made and how clients position themselves in the world with others. Humour is more of a complex process; it is the quality of being funny and is associated with laughter. Humour can be seen as an attempt to reduce the distance between people, but it also has the potential to alienate and shame, and so needs to be utilised with caution.

3.3   Are existential therapists empathic?

What is empathy?

Debating definitions of empathy are beyond the scope of this part. Instead, we shall use a definition created by Cuff and colleagues (2016) from their review of 43 distinct definitions of empathy. Cuff et al. described empathy as:

> an emotional response (affective), dependent upon the interaction between trait capacities and state influences. Empathic processes are automatically elicited but are also shaped by top-down control processes. The resulting emotion is similar to one's perception (directly experienced or imagined) and understanding (cognitive empathy) of the stimulus emotion, with recognition that the source of the emotion is not one's own.

So, it is not feeling what another feels through a magical, telepathic connection but instead, empathy is an act of imagination resulting from our similarities as human beings (Deurzen & Adams, 2016). Furthermore, how the therapist communicates empathy and how it is perceived by the client are factors most often associated with therapeutic outcomes (see Wampold, 2015).

Empathy is more than a technique; it is a way of being present. This was particularly explored in the work of Edith Stein, who was once a research assistant for Husserl. Stein was from a Jewish family but later converted to Catholicism and became a nun before being killed in Auschwitz. Empathy, according to Stein, is a distinctive intentional experience rather than a tool for understanding others. Although the contents of an empathic experience might arise as a result of being with others, Stein claimed that empathy is experienced first, personally. This account of empathy was quite revolutionary as Stein offered an account of empathy that did not describe empathy as being an experience of foreign consciousness. To feel the living experience of the other is different from knowing about the interior feelings of the other. Like the definition given at the start of this Part, empathy is the clear perception of the presence of the other in oneself and is a prerequisite for both knowledge of others and the self (McDaniel, 2016). This experience of being able to feel the other in us characterises the person and is constitutive of personhood; the state of being a person. For more on Edith Stein, see Section 5.2.

Existential empathy

Vanhooren and colleagues have differentiated between general empathy and existential empathy (2022). General empathy is directed towards the typical struggles and challenges in daily life; essentially general empathy is concerned with the ontic. Existential empathy, on the other hand, is concerned with the ontological, the experience of the human condition and this includes confrontations with ultimate concerns. More specifically, Vanhooren (2022) defines existential empathy as 'the capacity to be present, to resonate and to empathize with the client's existential concerns, and to communicate this empathy.'

However, the therapist and the client share the same existential concerns by way of being human, and as a consequence, the difference between the self and the other is harder to maintain. However, if the existential therapist can stay grounded within oneself and can be existentially empathic, a safe therapeutic space is created, and this may facilitate new meaning in life.

The importance of relating

Existential therapists have been greatly influenced by the work of the theologian and philosopher Martin Buber (1878–1965). In Buber's account of the relationships between people, human beings are described as having two distinct ways of relating to each other. The first of these, which Buber (1970) calls 'experience' (or the mode of 'I–it'), is the mode that is most often used in everyday life. In this mode, there is a distance between the experiencing *I* (the subject) and the experienced *It* (the object – the It). The subject is an objective observer rather than an active participant; this observer collects, analyses, and classifies data so that the object of the experience (the other) can be put to some purpose. This is the mode of experience we encounter every day when someone talks at us, rather than engages with us in a meaningful and shared dialogue.

However, there is also another mode of relating available to us which Buber called 'encounter' (the mode of 'I–Thou'). In this mode, we enter into a meaningful and real relationship, characterised by a fullness of being, and as a result, both the *I* and the *Thou* are transformed. The existential therapist aims to know another in this second mode of relating in which the person before us ceases to be an 'it' and instead becomes a 'thou.' Rather than knowing specific things about a client, the existential therapist will aim to grasp knowing and relating to their being. Schneider writes 'in order to "grasp the being" of the client, and consequently help the client "grasp her being," the therapist must bring a full and genuine presence to the therapeutic encounter' (2019, p. 254). In other words, to establish a real relationship, we strive to be fully open and present in attending to our clients.

3.4 Do existential therapists make interpretations?

Before we can clarify whether or not existential therapists interpret, we must define what an interpretation is. Interpretation is generally associated with psychoanalytic and psychodynamic approaches where it can be loosely defined as any communication made by the therapist to connect conscious (or preconscious) feelings, thoughts, and behaviours to unconscious factors. Interpretation is used primarily to promote insight but also as a tool for translation between different internal processes (Bateman et al., 2010). For example, as Rycroft describes:

> the analyst is someone who knows something of the way in which repudiated wishes, thoughts, feelings and memories can translate themselves into symptoms, gestures and dreams, and who knows, as it were, the grammar and syntax of such translations and is therefore in a position to interpret them back again into the communal language of consciousness.
>
> (1968, p. 18)

Of course, existential therapists do not hold the same view of consciousness and the unconscious as psychoanalytic practitioners might (see Section 2.2). Consciousness, from an existential perspective, is always directed towards something and can be either pre-reflective (that which we have not yet reflected on and maybe just out of awareness) or reflective (self-consciousness that is explicit, conceptual, and objectifying awareness).

However, broader definitions of interpretation exist in the literature. For example, Akhtar defines interpretation as referring to 'the analyst's verbally conveying to the patient his understanding of the patient's material' and also 'an unmasking and deciphering of activity' (2009, p. 466). This more general definition of deciphering activity will include all acts of inferring implicit meanings of behaviours and self-expression and not just those communications between therapist and client. As Schermer describes interpretation is 'a human experience necessitated by the depth, complexity, and concealment inherent in the personality and human affairs.... Rather, it is a ubiquitous aspect of human life' (2014, p. 6). This observation fits very well with Frankl's (1985) understanding of humans being intrinsically meaning creating beings; we naturally interpret the implied intentions and purposes of the behaviour of ourselves and others.

In existential therapy, we are always interpreting in this broader sense; we are always making sense of reality and discerning new meanings (Adams & van Deurzen, 2016). Interpretations though must be delivered as suggestions, as invitations to mutual explorations, and offered in the spirit of 'could it be that…?' or "I get the feeling that…' (Bateman et al., 2010).

Adams and van Deurzen (2016) describe four qualities of successful interpretations:

Simplicity

The therapist must state the interpretation tentatively but with clarity and firmly, encouraging clients to verify, correct, and refine.

Connectivity

The interpretation should be connected to a current preoccupation and the internal and external consequences it has in the client's life. By linking a present experience with the past and/or future-as-currently-lived and highlighting the client's active part in it, the client's sense of ownership and authorship is reinforced.

Coherence

Therapists must make interpretations from within the client's framework rather than their own theory. Entering willingly into a discussion when a client disagrees with an interpretation can help the client gain a focused view of their situation and promote the pleasure of probing and facing up to their existential situation.

Relevance

Timing is crucial; an interpretation made too early or too late will be irrelevant or distracting.

Existential therapy is a joint search for meaning and by making interpretations existential therapists can encourage a client to articulate their own living experiences while developing a capacity to make sense of and take ownership of their lives.

3.5   Do existential therapists work with the past?

In Section 1.5 we considered how existential therapists consider the past, present, and future as equally important in the understanding of human *Being*. Human existence cannot be understood without an understanding of how we live in time. In the present, there is an opportunity to reflect upon past patterns and face the future with courage.

The self

Sartre's (1943) assertions that we are 'condemned to be free' and 'existence precedes existence,' acknowledge the responsibility we each have for living authentically and creating ourselves. Sartre came to believe and outlined in *Being and Nothingness* that humans were no-thing, but pre-reflective consciousness. We are not concrete selves in the same way objects are; instead, we only exist in the moment and we are in a constant process of change, having to create ourselves every day. Therefore, selfhood in existential terms is dynamic and ever-changing; we are always in transformation and always able to reflect and take an understanding of our past. Because we retain the building materials and substances of selfhood from the continuous flux of life, our self is always temporary, easily altered, destroyed, and undermined by circumstances. As Deurzen further elaborates:

Although one person's building blocks are clearly different from another's for genetic and socio-cultural reasons. Out of the givens in and around us, we create a self. The self once created remains under construction and can be undone and rebuilt as circumstances and one's perception of who we want to be, change.

(2009, p. 166)

What is important to note is that our sense of self is connected to our freedom in that we feel most real when we are free to create and recreate ourselves, yet there are times in which we crave the certainty of choosing a specific role and way of being. It is easier to identify ourselves in particular ways because of our past experiences (e.g. as a victim, or aggressor). An existential therapist would work with a client to explore past experiences to break free from them and take ownership of past choices. It is through a developing self-awareness that new choices, commitments, and understandings of self are created. It is also worth mentioning here that clients may very well make choices comparable to what has already been chosen, but this is not the point; the point is that any choices made are owned (Adams & Deurzen, 2016).

Memories

It is often assumed that it is only psychoanalytic and psychodynamic approaches that work with the past. In these approaches, the role of the therapist is thought to be to uncover the 'truths' of the past so that present conflicts and issues can be understood and resolved in some way. However, Freud's understanding of the remembered past was more complex than that. As Conway (2006) describes, 'memories, then, are peculiar experience – near symbols of the self that both reveal and conceal goals, purposes, desires, and images of the self in the past.' Memories are not just simple fragments of past experience but are motivated by (unconscious or pre-reflective) goals and therefore will change. For example, the psychodynamic practitioner Michael Jacobs writes:

A person's history will change, sometimes subtly, sometimes with dramatic new revelations, as the person changes; and, in therapy, as the therapeutic relationship passes through its different phases. Sometimes there are new memories, but all the time there are possibilities of new interpretations, and fresh ways of constructing experiences. We are, in health, constantly interpreting and reinterpreting ourselves, our past and the present. It is a rigid view that is less healthy.

(Jacobs, 2012, p. 20)

Memories of the past then can confirm important aspects of our present understanding of ourselves. Spinelli writes 'the remembered past exposes, reflects and validates currently lived experiences' (2014, p. 54). In essence, memory is recognised in existential therapy to be fluid, based on present motivations, and consequently selective.

Past, present, and future

Perhaps where existential extends psychodynamic and psycho-analytic thinking is how memory relates to the future-directed aspirations. The connection is described well by Spinelli who sees the past as 'the past-as-currently-lived-and-future-directed' (2014, p. 54). Spinelli describes the case of a client exploring in therapy the notion that *I am always polite*. However, during the course of the therapy, in exploring and verifying this statement of self, memories of impoliteness are brought forward, and consequently, the notion that they are always polite is amended to *I am usually, but not always polite*. Furthermore, on more exploration of impoliteness and politeness, the client begins to understand something about their relationship to politeness and so an additional component emerges: *I will try to be polite even though sometimes I find it really difficult.* The remembered past, therefore, provides us with a means to validate our current sense of self but also describes whatever future direction we wish for. Cohn describes the existential position very well by stating 'the past is still present in a present that anticipates the future' (1997, p. 26).

3.6   How do existential therapists work with dreams?

Working with dreams has long been associated with psycho-analytic and psychodynamic practices, but existential therapists also have a long history of working with dreams; as such, they are invaluable assets in therapeutic practice.

Medard Boss and existential dream analysis

Medard Boss (1903–1990) was a Swiss psychiatrist and psycho-therapist who had first trained in Freudian psychoanalysis before becoming increasingly interested in existential philosophy and the work of Heidegger. In 1957, Boss published his form of exist-ential therapy termed Daseinanalysis, based on Heideggerian concepts like attunement, world openness, and embodiment, and in the same year published *The Analysis of Dreams.*

In this work, Boss rejected Freud's assumptions of the sym-bolism of dreams and instead considered a dream to be an expression of the dreamer's experience of existence. In this way, dreams are to be taken at face value with no differenti-ation between objective and subjective levels. As Cohn writes 'Dreams are an uncovering, an unveiling, and never a covering up' (1997, p. 84). It is through phenomenological exploration of the dream that the dreamer's current mode of being, world-views, beliefs, and fears can be uncovered (Iacovou & Weixel-Dixon, 2015). The same methods applied to dreams can also be applied to daydreams, and fantasies, as each has meaning in the same way, as an everyday experience.

How to work with a dream

Of course, as mentioned previously, there are no absolute rules, regulations, or prescribed techniques in existential therapy and so there is no way to phenomenological work with dreams. In this section, we will present three comparable descriptions of working with dreams.

Deurzen and existential structural analysis

Deurzen describes the aims of working with dreams as assisting 'the client in distilling the essential meaning from the reported experience, whether this experience was real or imagined' (2012, p. 170). However, she notes that it is essential that the client assigns meaning to the dream and not the therapist, even if the therapist can recognise potential meanings. In this way the client can act on any insight gained from the dream; meanings attributed by the therapist may be too premature for the client, and so the client will not be able to make use of the insight.

In this approach, the client is encouraged to explore their dream in the fullest way possible. Deurzen provides some simple guidelines to do this effectively. First of all the client is asked to carefully describe the dreams, several times in a row. The therapist does not make any interpretation, nor do they ask questions. In the second telling, the therapist might ask for clarifications but still does not impose meaning. At this point, the structural existential analysis begins and in this stage, the therapist and client will explore the dream using each dimension of the four worlds (see Section 2.8 for a description of the four worlds). In brief, these can be characterised as follows:

- On the physical dimension, the dreams' material world, objects, and sensations will be explored.
- On the social dimension, the dreams' social context will be explored. This includes a description of social roles and the nature of relationships.
- On the personal dimension, the private world implied in the dream is explored. This includes actions, motivations, intentions, desires, and objectives.
- On the spiritual dimension, the dreams' worldview will be explored. This may include kinds of morality displayed alongside values, assumptions, beliefs, and principles expressed.

In this description of working with dreams, Deurzen concludes that using the four worlds as a way of exploring dreams allows for an approach to living to be illustrated. As she writes 'working with dreams in this way is about allowing people to realise which images and fantasies about the world are holding them back, so that they get ready to start undoing these or complement them with more helpful ones' (Deurzen, 2012, p. 180).

Ernesto Spinelli and dream exploration

Spinelli views dreams as allowing the dreamer an opportunity to challenge current worldviews by providing dream-world alternatives to explore and play with. Spinelli (2014) describes the following steps in working with a dream:

1 The client is asked to recount the remembered dream in their own initially preferred way.
2 The client is then asked if there is any additional information that might be of immediate relevance to the dream.
3 The client is invited to consider the dream from several focused clarifications designed to contextualise the dream.

    a Spatial contextualising (the dream's setting)
    b Temporal contextualising (e.g. was it the present, past, or future?)
    c Contextualising dream-world objects (describing each dream-world object)
    d Contextualising the dreamer in the 'dream world' (describing the protagonist)
    e Contextualising key behaviour

4 The client is then asked to repeat the dream in the present tense.
5 The therapist will then repeat the dream in the present tense, using the first person (I...).

6 The client is asked if the repetition has evoked any further thoughts.

7 The therapist will then highlight key elements from an inter-relational perspective (ee.g. between protagonists or key dream-world objects).

8 Each of these key inter-relational dream elements will then be explored descriptively to explore dispositional stances.

9 With consideration of the discoveries of preceding stages, the inter-relations between dream-world elements will be explored.

10 Presenting problems of recent therapy sessions are then explored concerning what has emerged in the dream exploration.

11 Finally, the therapist and client will explore what has emerged in relation to fixed patterns of rigid dispositional stances (Spinelli terms this as sedimentations).

Like Deurzen, Spinelli (2014) highlights how while the client is challenged to clarify and describe their experience at no time should the therapist transform, distort, or add to the dream material. Spinelli adds the following:

> My personal view is that dreams permit clients to address difficult concerns and issues from the initially more secure and distanced 'third-person' perspective of 'the dreamer in the dream.' In this partially dissociated manner, views, values, fears, and beliefs that would otherwise be difficult, if not impossible, to 'own' in the client's 'waking-life' worldview are permitted their expression and exploration.
>
> (2014, p. 159)

Darren Langdridge and existential dream analysis

In the vein of Deurzen and Spinelli, Langdridge (2018) highlights how exploring dreams can gain insight into current ontic concerns. He writes 'dreams offer an imaginative space unfettered by the everyday demands/limits of conscious being-in-the-world, in which all four dimensions might be present without inhibition' (Langdridge, 2018, p. 59). Unlike Deurzen and Spinelli however, instead of proposing a stepped approach, Langdridge critically interrogates the dream story across 'fractions of the lifeworld' (Ashworth, 2016). These fractions are mutually dependent dimensions of the lifeworld and are drawn from ideas from Husserl, Heidegger, Merleau-Ponty, and Sartre. For Langdridge perhaps the most relevant to therapy is the fraction of selfhood – the subjective understanding of who we are. By critically exploring selfhood in dreams, by asking questions such as who is the dreamer, what do we make of them, what aspect of life does this sense of identity open up or close down, a client can play with an identity. As Langdridge states working in this way 'offers a safe space to come face-to-face with existential limits around selfhood and identity' (2018, p. 61).

In all three descriptions of working with dreams, the phenomenological approach is used to elucidate the meanings of dreams as they apply to a dreamer's current mode of being, worldviews, beliefs, and fears. As Cohn states, dreams 'are not puzzles to be solved but openings to be attended to' (1997, p. 84).

3.7 How do existential psychotherapists work with difference?

When working with others, social, cultural, and ethical issues are always present. Culture in particular influences language and creative expression. The existential philosopher Merleau-Ponty (1945), in his book *The Phenomenology of Perception*, described how culture provides the 'available meanings' and in doing so, constrains possibilities of meaning and subsequently their expression. Merleau-Ponty used the term sedimentation to refer to the process in which culture acts to shut down meaning. While we live, we take on information about our bodies and environment so that we can act intelligently without much effort or attention. Merleau-Ponty used the analogy of a river accumulating particles as it flows and depositing them as sedimented structures which then direct the river's flow. And so, the information we gain as we live gradually builds and guides our behaviour.

This can be applied to all contexts including mental health where it may influence the help-seeking behaviour of clients as well as the clinician's practice. As part of continuing professional and personal development, all practitioners should continue to develop their competence in addressing cultural differences and diversity. By becoming more aware of our own cultural beliefs and values and how these may be different from other cultures, we are more able to care for clients with diverse values, beliefs, and behaviours.

Existential philosophy, while emphasising choice and freedom, has long recognised that not all human beings are always free to choose. We are thrown into being in the world without a choice of where we land. We are thrown into a particular body, time, and culture and each will influence how far our freedom extends. Cohn described this very well in the following: 'Our thrownness is the unchosen basis on which our freedom to make choices rests' (1997, p. 96). (See Section 1.5 for a consideration of the concept of thrownness.) It is beyond this particular text to adequately describe diversity in depth, but it is useful to consider two aspects in order to explore what might be therapeutic.

Simone de Beauvoir and gender

Simone de Beauvoir was an existential thinker whose thinking greatly influenced the feminist movement. In one of her most famous books, *The Second Sex*, Beauvoir argues that men fundamentally oppress women by defining them exclusively in opposition to men and characterising them as 'other,' inessential, and incomplete, on every level. In doing so, man denies the humanity of women. In exploring the source of this imbalance, Beauvoir concludes that the disciplines of biology, psychoanalysis, and historical materialism revealed indisputable 'essential' differences but provided no justification for women's inferiority. However, this was taken for granted and perpetuated throughout human development. As a result, women are not born 'feminine' but shaped by a thousand external processes and, at each stage, women are conditioned into accepting passivity, dependence, repetition, and inwardness. Beauvoir famously stated that 'One is not born, but rather becomes, a woman' (1973, p. 301) to illustrate the process of how every force in society conspires to deprive woman of subjectivity and flatten her into an object. Denied the possibility of independent work or creative fulfilment, the woman must accept a dissatisfying life of housework, childbearing, and sexual slavishness. Once a woman loses her reproductive capacity, she loses her primary purpose and therefore her identity.

In essence, Beauvoir claims that woman's situation is not a result of her character. Rather, her character is a result of her situation. Her mediocrity, complacency, lack of accomplishment, passivity – all these qualities are the consequences of her subordination, not the cause. However, Beauvoir also describes how females are complicit in their Otherness, particularly regarding marriage. In this respect, Beauvoir sees women accepting the usual unfulfilling roles of wife and mother in order to achieve some security and comfort. Females are subordinated through this dependence and it is only by being able to financially support herself through work outside the home that a woman can achieve some autonomy and liberation.

Black existentialism

Black existentialism or *Africana critical theory* is a critical transformation of European existential ideas and their application to the experience of people of colour. Black existentialism shares many of the same concerns as (white) European existentialism, but there are differences between them. Philosophers such as Aime Césaire, Frantz Fanon, George Lamming, Wilson Harris, W. E. B. Du Bois, James Baldwin, Lewis Gordon, and Ralph Ellison argue that there are many instances where people of colour are prevented from living life as individuals. For example, black Americans are often treated by society as one homogenous group. Black existentialism has contributed much to discussions around mainstream notions of freedom and choice.

Central to Black existentialism is the concept of 'double consciousness'; a term originally conceptualised by Du Bois (1903) and found in his book *The Souls of Black Folk*. Essentially, Du Bois describes double consciousness as the internal conflict experienced by subordinated or colonised groups in an oppressive society. Double consciousness is the experience of 'always looking at one's self through the eyes' of a racist white society and 'measuring oneself by the means of a nation that looked back in contempt' (Du Bois, 1903).

Franz Fannon (1952) also touched upon ideas of double consciousness in his book, *Black Skin, White Masks*. Fanon expresses his hopelessness at being neither white nor black. Fanon identifies the double consciousness that African Americans face and its source; he claimed the cultural and social confusions of African Americans were the result of European culture and European history. This leads to many colonised peoples attempting to assimilate into whiteness, while others attempt to reject white European culture entirely; although Fanon did not approve of either approach. In seeking white acceptance, one must see whiteness as a standard, or the measure by which one should be judged; Fanon counselled against this, arguing that African Americans need to be educated to *not* follow the stereotypes determined by white culture.

The idea of double consciousness is important because it illuminates the experiences of people of colour living in post-colonised countries, and also because it sets a framework for understanding the position of oppressed people in an oppressive world. As a result, it became used to explain the dynamics of gender, colonialism, xenophobia, and more alongside, race. Indeed, double consciousness has been expanded to include other intersectional identities. This has been termed 'triple consciousness.' For example, women of colour not only have to see themselves through the lens of blackness and whiteness, but also through the lens of patriarchy.

Existential therapy and difference

Existential therapy is a predominately descriptive-focused practice that holds the premise that 'existence precedes essence.' As mentioned elsewhere, this means that we are nothing until we choose to act and it is in this way that we come into existence. An existential therapist will not seek to correct the experiences of a client but rather explore the experience of *being*. It is important to understand how the client experiences themselves in all aspects; from those elements that are beyond control and choice as well as those in which there is agency. Because the focus is on the experience of the client, 'existential psychotherapy does not merely tolerate but, more correctly, values and embraces the diversity of client worldviews as expressed in terms of culture, race, gender and sexual orientation' (Spinelli, 2014, p. 91).

3.8 Is it possible to have short-term existential therapy?

Time-limited, brief, or short-term therapy is considered to be between any number of sessions from 6 to 24; with the exact number usually being agreed upon by the client and practitioner. Though for many practitioners, open-ended or long-term therapy may be preferable, there are pragmatic reasons for briefer courses of therapy such as practical and economic constraints. Furthermore, short-term work should not be considered an inferior substitute. It is possible to have effective short-term existential psychotherapy. Rayner and Vitali (2016) conducted a study with 52 working-age people referred to their general practitioner for psychological intervention for depression and/or anxiety. Participants of the study completed a course of six phenomenologically informed therapy sessions, over a period of 12 weeks and reported significant reductions in the symptomology of depression and/or anxiety.

Like most aspects of existential practice, there is a sparseness in literature which perhaps can be explained by the reluctance to be constrained by rigid timescales or objectives (Cooper, 2003) and a general feeling that the dilemmas and challenges of life cannot be fixed quickly (Deurzen, 2012). From this perspective, it can be hard to see how a time-limited existential therapy will significantly address problems with living. However, in 1997 Strasser and Strasser emphasised the unique opportunities and potential afforded in a time-limited existential framework in their book titled *Existential Time-Limited Therapy: The Wheel of Existence.*

One of these potential opportunities is that short-term existential therapy allows an engagement with the existential givens of temporality and finitude. In this way, temporality can be used as leverage in the work 'the one important distinguishing feature of time-limited therapy is the limitation of time itself. So although the goal is to achieve the same kind of awareness as outlined in an open-ended approach, the aspect of time becomes a tool in itself' (Strasser & Strasser, 1997, p. 13). With a definitive end date a 'pressure' is created characterised by a more vital and urgent atmosphere that is advantageous for change. Making the client aware of the diminishing time facilitates a focus on outcomes and achieving objectives. Furthermore, as Strasser and Strasser highlight

…the simple fact of knowing that there is an ending tends to evoke stronger emotions… so, for instance, emotions such as fear, anger, sadness and the recollection of previous losses and rejections help clients to identify their value and coping strategies.

(1997, p. 15)

Another advantage of a pressured environment highlighted by Strasser and Strasser is that there is more likely to be a higher frequency of challenges and clarifications during the sessions than in open-ended therapy. The authors argue that this way of working 'catapults the client into self-disclosure and working more assiduously on issues' (ibid., p. 14).

Strasser and Strasser highlight that there should be no specific targets or goals in short-term existential therapy because all issues are 'inextricably linked' (ibid., p. 15). However, some therapists disagree. For example, Langdridge describes a 'tighter' focus when solution-focused approaches are incorporated into time-limited existential practice. This focus on future solutions is desirable, indeed 'may well be...appropriate' (Langdridge, 2006, p. 365). In essence, there is a sense of urgency that is characteristic of time-limited approaches that can be beneficial in the facilitation of a more favourable engagement with future living.

One of the applications of short-term existential work is in addressing substance misuse; indeed the Substance Abuse Mental Health Services Administration in the United States (Barry, 1999) recommended humanistic and existential time-limited approaches as being especially suitable for working with substance addictions. The report describes how emphasising the early development of the therapeutic relationship, the engendering of self-awareness, resilience, and resourcefulness empowers the client by encouraging a sense of choice and responsibility. It should be noted that while the protocol suggests that existential and humanistic time-limited approaches are compatible with 12-step programmes, since the emphasis is on acceptance of things that cannot be changed and the courage to make the changes that can be, the phenomenological philosophical underpinnings of an existential approach are at odds with the medical model and the consideration of addiction as a disease such as the 12-step programmes run by Alcoholics Anonymous (see Section 2.5).

3.9 What could you expect from an existential therapist in the first session?

It is quite usual in the first session of psychotherapy for the clinician to conduct an assessment. However, assessment is not a term that easily fits into existential practice. As Cohn (1997) highlights, assessment is not possible because there is nothing to assess, and furthermore assessing a client would inevitability establish the therapist as the leader of the therapeutic endeavour. Though an existential therapist may eventually frame a client's concerns using an existential lens (see Section 5.1 for more details), the first meeting is an opportunity to discover whether the therapist and the client are willing to work together.

To this end, there are several tasks the therapist will complete in the first session. These include

1 The establishment of a connection and rapport.
2 Gaining a measure of how the client thinks and feels about their presenting issues.
3 Gaining an understanding of why the client has decided to seek therapy now and not earlier?
4 Gaining an understanding of the client's ability to be challenged about their worldview and assumptions.
5 Thinking about the issues brought through an existential lens. This may be through a thoughtful reflection of the four worlds or maybe a consideration of the ultimate concerns of existence. What is over-represented or under-represented?
6 Monitoring their reaction or bias towards the client as they recall their experience.
7 Coming to a tentative conclusion about how the sessions might proceed. This might include a consideration of the number of sessions and availability.

8 Deciding whether the issues presented are in concordance with skill level. For example, novice practitioners may decide to refer onward if they feel the presenting issues are too complex for them.

9 Completing administrative tasks such as contracting, frequency, and fees.

In addition, the practitioner may explain their perspective on therapeutic work. While it is noted generally useful to talk about theory or existential philosophy, clients must have an understanding of how existential therapy is a collaborative endeavour designed to clarify the things that matter in creating a meaningful life. The client may subsequently have some questions about continuing onward, which the therapist should answer as best as they can. It is generally considered a good practice to provide the client with a clear information leaflet which could include qualifications, professional bodies, locations and timings, fees, conditions of payment, cancellation, and confidentiality policies.

Towards the end of the session, the therapist may ask the client about their feelings about the session, and the client may be encouraged to spend some time thinking about whether they wish to proceed. Perhaps assessment in an existential setting can, as Iacovou and Weixel-Dixon (2015) highlight, be seen as the opportunity for both client and therapist to check out and assess how well they can work with each other. It is noted though that this consideration should be an integral part of the ongoing therapy and not just a one-time event.

3.10 What is the difference between existential therapy and existential coaching?

Coaching is a vastly growing practice despite only having emerged as a profession relatively recently in contrast to therapy. The profession is largely credited to Timothy Gallwey's publication *The Inner Game of Tennis* in 1975 and it changed the field of sports coaching by encouraging athletes to work holistically to overcome mental blocks. The profession came to fruition in the 1980s when the motivational and aspirational elements of sports coaching were applied to organisational settings as well as life coaching.

Existential coaching emerged from general coaching practice and existential psychotherapy and combines the pragmatic, focused elements of coaching with the phenomenological work of existential practice. Clients are encouraged to identify and set goals, to self-reflect, and take a philosophical approach to life. Some existential coaches may apply additional tools from other coaching paradigms such as Neuro-linguistic programming (NLP) or solution-focused coaching, or they may remain with a purely phenomenological approach.

How does it differ from existential therapy?

In a nutshell, existential coaching is more future-focused. It assumes that there is a certain robustness in the client, so the focus is on the future and self-actualisation as opposed to the exploration of past and present experiences that characterise existential psychotherapy. Existential coaching is a reflective space that is designed to support clients in taking steps towards a desired direction. Sessions will include an exploration into a person's life and work predicament at the deepest possible level so that they can find their roots in their inner world, their picture of life, of the world, of themselves, and of the values and ideals they want to live by.

It encourages people to feel deeply, not only to explore the whole range of their bodily sensations, but to free their emotions, whether they are positive or negative, so that they are better able to plunge deeply into their thoughts. As Deurzen and Deurzen-Smith (2018, 120) describe:

> The transformation thus achieved by existential coaching is to move the person from having aspirational objectives

to having more inspirational objectives and from having a short term here and now view of the world to living in time, valuing past, present, future and eternity equally.

Because existential coaching is rooted in philosophy, clients are encouraged to think beyond the next milestone or goal and instead consider their overarching values and how they make meaning in the world. Goals are fluid, and this is to be expected given that existential philosophy challenges the human desire to become fixed entities. While an existential coach may encourage emotional exploration and making sense of past experiences, there is a sense of momentum in that an understanding of the past helps inform life choices going forward.

Existential coaching encourages the need to think holistically about oneself and enquire deeply about what matters. In essence, being rooted in the existential notions of freedom, choice, bad faith, and inauthenticity, existential coaching provides a space for people to think about the direction they take in life. Like existential psychotherapy, existential coaching encourages existential resilience and self-knowledge from directly challenging aspects of living. In this way, clients can make more authentic choices about how they want to live and advance in spite of the uncertainties, challenges, and complexities of life. If existential psychotherapy shows us that struggling is human and not a result of illness or deficiency, then existential coaching shows us that thriving is complex and impermanent.

Settings and application of existential coaching

As existential philosophy is all about the experience of being human, existential coaching is relevant to any setting. In organisations, coaches may explore the tension between the values of the individual and the values of the team, notions of authenticity at work, or how responsibility is avoided. An existential career coach might look at the inevitable anxiety of the freedom of choosing a new path, or how our sense of temporality impacts the urgency or guilt felt in response to making life choices. In life coaching, the possibilities are often much more open-ended as the work takes a holistic free-flowing approach and this is particularly useful for clients who perhaps have undertaken psychotherapy in the past and want a similarly safe and reflective space, but with a future-focused lens.

Further reading

Adams, M., & Deurzen, E. van (2016). *Skills in Existential Counselling & Psychotherapy*. Sage.

Cohn, H.W. (1997). *Existential Thought and Therapeutic Practice: An Introduction to Existential Psychotherapy*. Sage.

Deurzen, E. van (2012). *Existential Counselling & Psychotherapy in Practice*. Sage.

Deurzen, E. van, & Arnold-Baker, C. (2018). *Existential Therapy: Distinctive Features*. Routledge.

References

Adams, M. (2013). *A Concise Introduction to Existential Counselling*. Sage.

Adams, M. (2019). Existential-phenomenological therapy: Method and practice. In E. van Deurzen, E. Craig, A. Laengle, K.J. Schneider, D. Tantam, & S. du Plock (Eds.), *The Wiley World Handbook of Existential Therapy*. John Wiley & Sons, 167–180.

Adams, M., & Deurzen, E. van (2016). *Skills in Existential Counselling & Psychotherapy*. Sage.

Akhtar, S. (2009). *Comprehensive Dictionary of Psychoanalysis*. Routledge.

Ashworth, P.D. (2016). The lifeworld – Enriching qualitative evidence. *Qualitative Research in Psychology, 13*(1), 20–32.

Barry, K.L. (1999). *Tip 34: Brief Intervention and Brief Therapies for Substance Abuse: Treatment Improvement Protocol (TIP), Series 34*. Center for Substance Abuse Treatment, Rockville.

Bateman, A., Brown, D., & Pedder, J. (2010). *Introduction to Psychotherapy: An Outline of Psychodynamic Principles and Practice*. Routledge.

Beauvoir, S. de (1973). *The Second Sex*. Vintage Books.

Buber, M. (1970). *I and Thou* (vol. 243). Simon and Schuster.

Cohn, H.W. (1997). *Existential Thought and Therapeutic Practice: An Introduction to Existential Psychotherapy*. Sage.

Conway, M. (2006). Special issue: Memory and desire – Reading Freud. *The Psychologist*, 18 September. Retrieved from www.bps.org.uk/psychologist/special-issue-memory-and-desire-reading-freud

Cooper, M. (2003). Between freedom and despair: Existential challenges and contributions to person-centered and experiential therapy. *Person-Centered and Experiential Psychotherapies*, *2*(1), 43–56.

Cuff, B.M.P., Brown, S.J., Taylor, L., & Howat, D.J. (2016). Empathy: A review of the concept. *Emotion Review, 8*(2), 144–153.

Deurzen, E. van (2009). *Everyday Mysteries: A Handbook of Existential Psychotherapy*. Routledge.

Deurzen, E. van (2012). *Existential Counselling & Psychotherapy in Practice*. Sage.

Deurzen, E. van, & Arnold-Baker, C. (2018). *Existential Therapy: Distinctive Features*. Routledge.

Deurzen, E. van, & Deurzen-Smith, S. van (2018). Existential transformative coaching: Working with images, feelings and values to revitalize the life-world. *Existential Analysis*, *29*(1), 105–122.

Du Bois, W. (1903). *The Souls of Black Folk: Essays and Sketches*. A. C. McClurg & Co.

Fannon, F. (1952). *Black Skin, White Masks*. Grove Press.

Frankl, V.E. (1985). *Man's Search for Meaning*. Simon and Schuster.

Gibson, N., & Tantam, D. (2017). The best medicine? The nature of humour and its significance for the process of psychotherapy. *Existential Analysis: Journal of the Society for Existential Analysis*, *28*(2), 272–288.

Husserl, E. (1900). *Logical Investigations* (J.N. Findlay, trans.). Routledge (1970).

Iacovou, S., & Weixel-Dixon, K. (2015). *Existential Therapy: 100 Key Points and Techniques*. Routledge.

Jacobs, M. (2012). *The Presenting Past*. McGraw-Hill Education.

Langdridge, D. (2006). Solution focused therapy. *Existential Analysis: Journal of the Society for Existential Analysis*, *17*(2) 359–370.

Langdridge, D. (2018). Existential dream analysis. In S. du Plock (Ed.), *Case Studies in Existential Therapy: Translating Theory into Practice*. PCCS Books, 56–70.

May, R. (1981). *Freedom and Destiny*. W. W. Norton & Co.

McDaniel, K. (2016). Edith Stein: On the problem of empathy. In Schliesser, E. (Ed.), *Ten Neglected Classics of Philosophy*. Oxford University Press, 195–221

Merleau-Ponty, M. (1945). *Phenomenology of Perception*. Routledge.

Rayner, M., & Vitali, D. (2016). Short-term existential psychotherapy in primary care: A quantitative report. *The Journal of Humanistic Psychology*, *56*(4), 357–372.

Rycroft, C. (1968). *Psychoanalysis Observed*. Penguin.

Sartre, J-P. (1943). *Being and Nothingness – An Essay on Phenomenological Ontology* (H. Barnes, trans.). Philosophical Library (1956).

Schermer, V.L. (2014). *Meaning, Mind, and Self-Transformation: Psychoanalytic Interpretation and the Interpretation of Psychoanalysis*. Routledge.

Schneider, K.J. (2019). Existential-humanistic and existential-integrative therapy. In E. van Deurzen, E. Craig, A. Laengle, K.J. Schneider, D. Tantam, & S. du Plock (Eds.), *The Wiley World Handbook of Existential Therapy*. John Wiley & Sons. 247–256.

Spinelli, E. (2006). Existential psychotherapy: An introductory overview. *Análise Psicológica*, 3 (XXIV), 311–321.

Spinelli, E. (2014). *Practising Existential Therapy: The Relational World*. Sage.

Strasser, F., & Strasser, A. (1997). *Existential Time-Limited Therapy: The Wheel of Existence*. John Wiley.

Vanhooren, S. (2022). Existential empathy: The challenge of 'being' in therapy and counseling. *Religions*, *13*(8), 1–11. https://doi.org/10.3390/rel13080752

Vanhooren, S., Conrado Veiga Bosquetti, Y., & Frediani, G. (2022). The development of the existential empathy questionnaire. *Journal of Humanistic Psychology*, 00221678221144599.

Wampold, B.E. (2015). How important are the common factors in psychotherapy? An update. *World Psychiatry*, *14*(3), 270–277. https://doi.org/10.1002/wps.20238

Yalom, I. (1980). *Existential Psychotherapy*. Basic Books.

Part 4

Existential applications in different contexts

Questions about how the existential approach can be used for different presenting issues and client groups

Nancy Hakim Dowek

4.1 How do you formulate a case in existential therapy?

Existential therapy is rooted in the understanding that the clients' challenges are experienced through their own perspective, their lived experiences, and their subjective interpretation of it. These are approached with respect and validated by the therapist whilst exploring different possibilities and perspectives for interpreting these experiences.

Before going further, let us clarify what we mean by a formulation of a client case. The term 'conceptualisation' provides a means for abstract, reflective thinking; therefore, a case conceptualisation focuses on an overall understanding of the case through the lens of a particular theoretical orientation; in this case the existential lens. A case formulation is a conceptualisation, which includes additional information, such as the clients' history, diagnosis, and outcome goals. In a phenomenological analysis, the existential conceptualisation is initiated principally by what and how the client is operating, and focuses its attention on their capacity for confronting and addressing their existential challenges and needs (Felder & Robbins, 2021). Both are attained through a process of clarification, creating a

DOI: 10.4324/9781003355700-5

representation of the client's whole existence, which includes their existential drives and their capacity to encounter themselves and the world. In so doing, it is important to grasp the level of the disruption these personal difficulties or perceptions are creating and their impact on the individual on all dimensions of existence: physical, personal, social, and spiritual. The therapist will facilitate questioning of all these considerations and will explore obstacles and dangers in accordance with the expectations of the therapy.

Existential philosophy draws its vision from the understanding that human existence has universal aspects and challenges which are shared by all; Yalom (1980) describes these as the Givens of Existence. However, these common aspects and challenges are approached differently by each individual. Therefore, it could be argued that structuring an approach to case formulation and planning the therapeutic work of existential therapy may hinder the practice of the phenomenological and existential approach to therapy. However, despite the wisdom of keeping an open mind in the encounter between therapist and client, we need to be able to create a framework for the therapeutic process, and through that to enable communication between therapists and clients and therapists and supervisors. Such a framework can be revisited as a reference point for adjustment on a regular basis (Hoffman & Cleare-Hoffman, 2017).

How do we conceptualise clients' worlds and their relationships with the world around them without interpreting the clients experience and without acting as an expert; but rather as a meeting with the client wherever they are and accompanying them in their exploration of their lives? We need to bear in mind that focusing on a concept rather than the clients experience may become a slippery slope to pathologising and determining their way of being-in-the-world that may hinder the phenomenological focus and limit our perspective on emerging concerns and themes (Deurzen, 2012).

There are a few considerations and guidelines that will help keep the formulation expressed in line with existential and phenomenological philosophy while keeping the formulation as close as possible to the clients' experience. But we still need to set the parameters of the case formulation in order to reach a broader understanding of how to manage the therapeutic work. First, we need to uncover what is troubling the client, where their struggle lies, or what difficulty they are facing. Whilst doing this the focus is on the client's subjective experiences and use of their language. This will root us in the client's world and avoid useless theorising of the case we are formulating. For instance, it is better to avoid directly referring to a diagnosis, but where necessary, it is best to discuss this openly with the client so that we have an account of their experience of living with the diagnosed condition, rather than simply using a definition from the *Diagnostic and Statistical Manual of Mental Disorders*, a diagnostic tool published by the American Psychiatric Association (2013) (DMS). Their subjective and lived experience will be a determinant factor in formulating the client's case. To begin, an existential therapist will map the terrain of the client's world using the four dimensions of existence. Evaluating the strengths and limitations in each dimension and getting a sense of where the struggle lies and how different dimensions interact with each other for the client.

We will need to add more details to the formulation, such as the client's ability to be self-aware, their perspective of their problems or what they perceive to be their problems, and what meaning they are ascribing to them.

Once a map of the client's lifeworld has been created, it can be further elaborated through an examination of the client's experience through the givens of existence; that is, where is the client positioned existentially? The givens of existence will focus on such aspects as their freedom, isolation, meaninglessness, and death (Yalom, 1980). Is the client able to make sense of their narrative? If so, how? Is the client able to take responsibility for their choices, are they aware that they have choices? How do they interact with their therapist? How do they relate to therapy; what is their understanding of it? How do they describe their relationships, and how does that connect with the relationship they need to forge with their therapist? Are there emerging patterns? The existential therapist will also be keeping track of the values and beliefs that the client expresses and how these highlight what is important for the client but also how it can lead to assumptions and bias in their view of the world and themselves. Equally important however is that, throughout, the therapist should be aware of their own biases and interpretations, and their ability to bracket them.

Gaining a map of the client's lifeworld and their existential position in it will give an indication of what the client needs to address in order to live life in a better way. Using the existential givens and staying as close as possible to these, combined with the clients' experience in their own words, will help the therapist stay on track in their formulation.

4.2   Is existential therapy helpful for clients suffering from depression and high levels of anxiety?

Existing in the world entails confronting the givens of existence which have profound impacts on an individual's ability to understand themselves, their position with the world around them, and their relationships with others.

Existential anxiety originates from different aspects of existence. It is the result of the struggles individuals encounter when faced with the ultimate concerns of death, isolation, freedom, and meaninglessness (Yalom, 1980). It is an inherent aspect of being-in-the-world stemming from our quest to find meaning in life in light of the certainty of death and is rooted in the realisation that life is inevitably moving towards death (Heidegger, 1996) Anxiety is also rooted in our *thrownness*, which Heidegger (1996) conceptualised as being thrown into a world we did not choose, and into a reality and circumstances outside our control. Finally, anxiety is rooted in the necessity to make choices (even not making a choice is a choice), but the outcomes of which are never certain. It also always implies the rejection of alternatives and involves individuals to bear consequences that they will be responsible for (Sartre, 1966).

Confronted with the circumstances surrounding us as described earlier, the knowledge that the end result of life is known from its start and trying to make sense of our own experience within the limitations of these external structures, we start the struggle to make meaning. A struggle that will inevitably impact us and which can spark anxiety and depression (Temple & Gall, 2018). Yet, most people are disconnected from the concept and understanding of existential anxiety, therefore they look for external answers and adopt external rules and social guidelines for living their lives. Paradoxically, when anxiety is left unattended and unresolved, it grows and the individual starts experiencing a dissonance between their actions and their inner core values (Deurzen, 2012). They effectively step into inauthentic living, increasing the levels of anxiety, and the loss of meaning resulting in a sense of depression and personal anxiety. In that respect, both anxiety and depression are intertwined and cohabit alongside each other.

Depression is not an unfortunate occurrence, nor can it simply be dismissed as a chemical imbalance. It is the result of the inability to confront existence and its challenges on an ontological dimension. It is often the result of a limited world view and the avoidance of existential anxiety in particular. It originates from reflections on life leading to a sense of meaninglessness and emptiness which in turn may lead to feelings of desperation. The answers do not lie with finding the meaning *of* life but rather the meaning *in* life; the meaning we can find which infuses our personal life. As such, it needs to be addressed through the exploration of the clients' world view which has the potential for uncovering a new and more authentic view of existence.

We have established that anxiety is built into the experience of human existence. This existential anxiety, which is ontological by nature (meaning it is a universal aspect of existence experienced by all humans), is the origin of worries and anxieties (Deurzen, 2012). While we all share this phenomenon, every person will experience it in their own personal and subjective way and will interpret it in different ways. Individuals, whether consciously or not, still experience the influence of existential anxieties.

Furthermore, existentialists view anxiety as fundamental in our making sense of the world, not one to be related to as a problem to eradicate (May, 2015) but rather seeing our ability to confront this given of existence as taking a step closer to living authentically. May argued that anxiety is related to freedom and creativity, linked to our striving to become a self. Anxiety is not a negative to be overcome, but a force that can be channelled to live a meaningful life. Furthermore, without anxiety there would be no possibility and therefore no capacity to grow and develop as a human being (Kierkegaard, 2014).

Recognising and acknowledging existential anxiety is in fact the beginning of our self-awareness. Anxiety is crucial to spiritual life. It is the starting point of a well-lived life and is something to be confronted with and examined and not removed in therapy (Kierkegaard, 2014).

All the above point towards the direction taken in working with clients suffering from anxiety or depression. The work will concentrate on exploring the client's experience of existential anxiety and more likely their avoidance of it reverting to worries and concrete anxieties about day-to-day life which will result in a loss of meaning and depression. Not only is the aim of therapy not to eradicate anxiety but to learn to be with anxiety and channel it into our growth process.

4.3   How does existential therapy conceptualise trauma?

Trauma, by its nature, is existential through the impact it has on the way individuals experiencing it encounter the world around them and their ability to make sense of it. As a result, it affects their self-understanding, and their sense of place in the world. As a consequence a therapeutic approach and understanding of trauma should be addressed through the existential dimensions.

How is trauma conceptualised in the existential paradigm and how does it relate to the givens of existence? Trauma is an overwhelmingly stressful and unusual event outside the range of usual human experience (Levine & Frederick, 1997). It involves some kind of violence, abuse, or loss that threatens death or injury to oneself or another and that resists one's capacity to process, make sense, or schematise the occurrence in typical or familiar ways (DuBose, 2010). The 'overwhelming' part of this definition refers to our response to the event and not only to the factual aspect of it. Therefore, trauma is not solely about the event, but it is mainly about the individual's subjective experience of it and their ability to find a way to make sense of it. Furthermore, Levine and Frederick (1997) maintain that focusing on the nature of the event alone is insufficient and suggest that it is equally important to address the response to the event. Different people will react differently to the same event.

Thus, we have established that trauma is not only the result of the moment the event occurred, but it is ignited by it. The traumatic event carries potential for intense overwhelming, disruptive responses. It is followed by an immediate response to the event with thoughts and emotions. Subsequently this subjective response starts crystallising, which may be followed by an enduring reaction which may or may not include a disruption to one's daily life and to a person's ability to make sense of their experience of being and their ability to relate to others.

Loss of meaning will confront the traumatised person with the givens of existence and with disillusion in their valued beliefs. It will cause the loss of the basic perception of a stable and predictable world. The veil of denial is ripped apart, which alters our sense of being in the world (Stolorow, 2007) and we must then face the undeniable possibility of existing in a universe which is random and unpredictable. We are groundless and thrown into a new world where fundamental meaning and relating systems are irreparably shattered (Greening, 1992). The loss of everyday life's so-called normal, which is one of the pillars upon which we understand the world and take for granted, is no longer part of the existential world of the traumatised person. The traumatised person will not only feel a divide between their previous way of being and their present, but they will also experience an incongruity between their own world and the normal world they once knew which coincided with the world of others (Stolorow, 2007). They will become aware that the world they experience is forever and fundamentally different from the world they experienced before the trauma. It is in that split between the two worlds, inhabited by the traumatised person, that loneliness and isolation take hold and where the person will experience their suffocating imprisonment and estrangement from others.

Another contributor to this loss of meaning is the disruption of temporality, a breakdown in the connection in time between past, present, and future which is indispensable for our ability to make sense of the world. The future and past are united in the present. Time serves as one of the scaffoldings upon which our sense of self is wrapped and contained. Indeed, the whole of our being is so connected to time that without it we may not have the foundation for understanding our own being. Without that unity we become frozen in a perpetual present, unable to create a sense of coherence and meaning in life.

Experiencing intense pain following a trauma is an emotional response to the process described before. However, pain is not pathology and the event itself is not the whole picture. It is in the absence of a relational context, a space in which the individual is heard, held, validated, and understood, that causes the trauma to form in the traumatised individual's mind. In fact, by looking at trauma just as the result of an event is reductionist, it invalidates the experience and removes all control or responsibility from the traumatised person, leaving them lost and helpless in a world that does not make sense. Hence, obstructing the pathway leading to understanding and healing.

The psychotherapeutic relationship involves the validation and the value of the individual's unique way of being. It entails a therapeutic process of shared discovery in which the meaning of the client's lived experience is explored, understood, and eventually transformed. The exploration is about the subjective experience of the client and not about pathologising or labelling them. On the contrary, it is all about understanding, attentiveness, and acceptance, and acknowledging the existential shattering experienced by the traumatised person. Paradoxically, it is the unveiling of our human vulnerability that brings to the forefront the possibility of authenticity and determination. Truly courageous exploration and re-evaluation of values, beliefs, and their social context would provide an opportunity for expanding the sense of self.

4.4   How do existential therapists work with clients diagnosed with life limiting or terminal illness?

Terminally ill patients or individuals with limiting illnesses are frequently confronted with severe existential aspects of their human existence and their limitations. Confronting the givens of existence in such a situation can create extremely distressing existential and spiritual suffering for terminally ill individuals or those chronically limited by illness. Both cases will highlight the tension between facticity, limitations, and freedom.

Therefore, the importance of support and therapy during this time is invaluable. It is important to acknowledge that at this stage the whole individual is affected by their condition on all dimensions: physical, personal, and social relational difficulties towards self and others and emotional issues, and on a spiritual level attempting to make sense and find meaning (Lima et al., 2014).

In addition, there is the overarching awareness of temporality in coming to terms with the past and present. Issues including integrity or regrets for unfulfilled needs or wishes; it is about a present that is overshadowed by a threatening and concretely limited future that may seem pointless and coloured by hopelessness and a loss of meaning. Also, the prospect of death may raise religious worries, regardless of religious beliefs or the lack of them that an individual is holding.

The work at this stage will start by creating a safe environment in which the client can find the space to explore their experience of being in the present, to move through the pain, explore and acknowledge the freedom to internally roam, and explore the possibility of accepting the limitations and possibilities (Deurzen, 2012).

Reasoning and emotions invariably overlap in the realm of meaning making. This means that the process of creating meaning becomes extremely important in the face of the many challenges that the client faces. Death punctuates life, it may destroy us physically but can save us spiritually (Yalom, 1980), since it provides a definite time frame that makes us realise the value of life; the value of the everyday and the importance of the way we are choosing to live our lives. Above all, it teaches that there are no infinite attempts at living. Death is no longer a nebulous and distant concept; it has been infused by a sense of urgency to uncover what can be uncovered as a choice and not one simply dictated by the circumstances. However, creating meaning in the face death or when facing life-changing illnesses can be a difficult and challenging task that may be seen by some as almost impossible; it requires mobilising existential courage and commitment, and above all it is a tale of ownership of one's life and existence. Being confronted by the experience of living towards death means not only taking stock and creating meaning of the experience of the temporal dimension, as mentioned earlier, but also the spatial dimension, that is, the embodiment of the lived experience, in a physical body.

Life is limited by definition, and we are all subject to our own *sell by* date, whether we are healthy or ill, or at the early stages of life, mid–stages, or at our end-of-life stage. However, we all go to great lengths to avoid that confrontation, which is no longer available to the life-limited and terminally ill individuals. Paradoxically, that confrontation opens the opportunity for honestly examining the life that we have lived and the way we would like to live our remaining time on earth.

This process can be productive for some people but can equally create feelings of anxiety and hopelessness that seem punishing and relentless. However, facing our own mortality and our limitations, especially at the end-of-life stage, is an opportunity to find ways of taking agency over one's lived life and exploring the relationship to self and others. Frankl (2014) argued that by creating meanings associated with suffering one may begin to actively engage in a response to living and dying. Instead of sinking into despair totally paralysed by anxiety, one could engage actively in the process of understanding the meaning of these feelings and by doing so infuse meaning into the process one finds oneself in.

Karl Jaspers (1970) proposed that to exist as an authentic being one must face limiting situations which include death, suffering, struggle, and guilt. Only by entering these limiting situations and digging deep within oneself to find the resources and strength and the limitless freedom to confront the challenges of existence can we step into our authentic dimension. We cannot hide from limiting situations therefore it necessitates a transcending movement of the self, a transformed way of existing in the world; existing as an authentic being. Illness is both a limiting situation but also its consequence (Campos-Winter, 2020).

Existential philosophers argued that existential anxiety is at the heart of the unease we experience when we become self-conscious and aware of our vulnerability and possible death and our freedom to live the time we have according to our own internal and authentic truth (Kierkegaard, Heidegger, Sartre). Existential guilt on the other hand is the guilt of all the lives we did not live and perhaps of our not having lived up to our potential. This is the responsibility which we carry towards ourselves.

Facing such challenges will inevitably generate anxiety for the client. The existential therapist will encourage clients to explore their individual experiences. Meaning is created when clients learn to identify aspects of themselves for which they were unaware, and which in turn will change their outlook on their life. Consequently, this will impact their future choices regardless of the length of their remaining time. This shift in perspective is at the heart of the creation of meaning for these clients.

4.5 What is the existential view of loss and bereavement?

Grief is an inescapable and universally shared experience; it is a natural response to the experience of loss. It is not possible to go through life without experiencing a series of losses, which may include a loss of identity, loss of good health, loss of home and country of origin and with it a cultural and emotional way of life, and of course it includes loss of loved ones through separation or death. The experience of grief is complex and occurs on multiple levels: emotional, cognitive, existential, and spiritual. It can trigger an existential crisis, resulting in the loss of all previous reference points which created meaning prior to this.

We all experience grief in different ways, based on our previous personal history, our lived experience, our beliefs, and our relationship with the person we have lost. We are all unique beings with a subjective perspective, with a unique history and therefore a unique way of making sense of reality, especially when we struggle to make sense of these. Existentially, bereavement is connected to fundamental aspects of existence. First, it is connected to death. One of the givens of existence relates to the limitation of every experience. Every start inherently contains its own ending. We may hold different relationships with life and death. However, we share a universal need to make sense of every experience in order to process them. This is even more pronounced when we are dealing with grief and bereavement, which not only involves the grief for the person we have lost but also anxiety relating to our own mortality.

Loss touches upon temporality, as the loss and bereavement disrupt the continuous connection with time. It impacts directly on the ability to picture a clear vision of the future, since this future does not include the person who died. It entails living with a past that is no longer concretely connected to the present and the future that we imagined included the person we lost. It reinforces the fact that the past is in the past, since the person we lost does not exist concretely in the present. Therefore, it has disrupted the possibility of a shared future with them, which in turn impacts on the loss of the constructed and familiar vision we had of the future.

Loss is directly linked to our relatedness to others in so far as each human existence essentially is an interaction with the wider world and interaction with others (Madison, 2005). Therefore, the bereaved person has lost part of their world and the way they perceived it.

Relatedness is experienced on multiple dimensions. And since we are embodied beings; we exist in our bodies and our physicality as part of our experience of being with ourselves and of being with others. Thus, the bereaved person has lost a part of their world, allegorically and literally. The bereaved person may retain a sense of connection experienced on a physical level with the person who died and exists no more. This physical connection was co-created in the interpersonal space within which they both lived. Thus, grief necessitates an adjustment to a new meaning of our own identity. As such grief work necessitates the transformation of meaning structures (Wong, 2010).

Yalom's (1980) view is that loss and bereavement can cause a rip in the fabric of our assumed world, through which unwelcome existential realities may be glimpsed which cannot be unseen. Thus, the bereaved person will have to recreate his understanding of the world which includes this existential reality through their work with their therapist.

However, the bond with the deceased person does not vanish because of their death. We do not stop loving people because they have died. Furthermore, sometimes the bereaved person will reshape their relationship with the deceased which indicates an active and continuous relationship with them. The continuing bonds theory (Klass & Stephan, 2018) radically swayed from the hegemony of pathologising grief based on Freudian model of bereavement (1957). It validated the experience of continuous bonds and argued that after their death the deceased person can still play a role, albeit differently, in lives of individuals and families.

In order to recreate a balance and address the void created by the loss of a loved one will require the process of an elaborate exploration of the experience for the bereaved person. Furthermore, the experience of loss could be an 'existential opportunity,' albeit a painful or even overwhelming one.

The therapy would address all four dimensions of existence (Deurzen, 2012) when working with a bereaved person. It is important not to pathologise grief, simply because it is present in one's life for a long period of time. It has its own dynamic which surges or subsides, especially at an anniversary or during special occasions. It is important to acknowledge that sometimes time does heal, but not completely. Working existentially with grief is also about holding the paradox of love and loss (Deurzen, 2023). It is about facing the pain instead of shutting it down and looking for ways to integrate that loss into life and accept it through creating a new sense of meaning and purpose (ibid.).

Therapy is about creating a safe space in which the bereaved person can explore phenomenologically the experience and its meaning to them, accompanying them and witnessing their pain and their sorrow, respecting their pace. Eventually it is about helping the grieving person making sense of this experience according to their own perspective and beliefs. That is not to say it cannot be challenged, but there is no prescriptive protocol to follow.

4.6 What is the existential perspective on addiction?

Addiction is a multi-layered phenomenon which includes psychological, social, legal, and existential layers, all intertwined with each other. It also includes a biological and neurological component. Therefore, addiction should not be considered in a reductive manner, exclusively in terms of physicality or in terms of behaviour. It is overall a much broader phenomenon and needs to be addressed as such. Since it implies a considerable loss of meaning; a loss of connection with self and with the individual's affective environment, a level of distress and struggles in the face of the existential givens (Carreno & Pérez-Escobar, 2019). It is not simply a disease or illness that finds its way into the individual's internal world, but rather a way of being and existing in the world and being and relating to others.

Existential philosophy and consequently existential psychotherapy explores the unavoidable aspects of human existence and suggests an approach for tackling and understanding questions of human struggles. It asks what is the meaning of life? What am I doing here? What is the point of living, and trying to strive and reach, if life inevitably ends in death? What is freedom of choice in light of the ultimate finitude of death? All of these fundamental questions are closely related to the experience of the addicted person.

Individuals can develop addiction as a result of different lived experiences and their struggle to make sense of them. It can be triggered by feeling alienated from self and others, but estrangement could be the result of the addiction as well. It could also be perceived as a strategy to escape from suffering and traumatic experiences. However, regardless of the causation, a person presenting with addictions will demonstrate existential conflicts and challenges such as meaninglessness, loneliness, death, guilt, and loss of control (Wiklund, 2008). It stems from the anxiety generated by the confrontation with the givens of existence and is amplified by it (Du Plexis, 2018). The meaning of life and the lack of it is one of the most central existential questions. When this question remains unanswered and when one does not have a clear purpose and motivation in life, one becomes detached from others, separated from society, and disengaged from their purpose and original project (Sartre, 1966). When there is a feeling that one's life is not worth living, the individual experiences an existential vacuum (Frankl, 2014) and this lack of meaning in life can result in addiction.

In addition, individuals who resort to addiction, struggle with the temporal dimensions of their existence in the world. They have trouble linking meaningfully, their present with their past and a vision of the possibilities their future holds. They have not been able to create an existential temporal framework to support and sustain them in times of crisis, which can be developed through existential therapy.

Another existential aspect of addiction is linked to the search for freedom and pushing boundaries, which paradoxically results in restricting the addicted person and shrinking their world. In fact, this lack of freedom is amplified by restricting the explanation of addiction to those deterministic formulations which view human conditions through rigid parameters such as physicality, emotions, cognitions, social context, etc. This rigid conceptualisation encourages looking for external causation and resolutions rather than looking for the answers internally. Frankl (2014) suggested that even in extremely restricted situations and profound suffering, there is always a degree of freedom situated in the choice of attitude we adopt towards that suffering. We always have choices. We always have the freedom to choose. Avoidance of taking ownership of the freedom that we have is strongly present in addiction. People with addiction have a tendency to attach the reasons for their situation onto external factors and they may consider their addiction to be stronger than their own power. Furthermore Boss (1983) suggested that addiction, in whatever form, is always the result of a desperate search, on a deceptive misleading and hopeless path, for the realisation of human freedom.

As a result of the complexity described earlier, working with clients with addiction requires a holistic approach, addressing the overall experience of the addicted person and which should touch upon all four dimensions of existence (Deurzen, 2012): physical, psychological, interpersonal problems, and spiritual dimensions that have been initially created or resulted as a consequence of the addiction.

Thus, it is imperative that the therapist accompanying and supporting those requiring help with addictions should address the whole person and not the addiction as a separate phenomenon. Addiction as a standalone condition does not exist. It is rather a real and unique person, with a whole unique lived experience and unique personal history who is experiencing difficulties and struggling to find his/her place in the world.

Conceptualising addiction as the result of difficulties confronting the existential struggles of life, and including the real lived experience of the addict, allows the process in the therapy room to preserve the person's dignity and humanity whilst relating to the person as a capable human being who can, through engaging with these struggles, navigate their lives in new ways, while taking responsibility for the choices and finding a way of infusing meanings into their lives.

4.7   How do existential therapists work with clients with auditory and visual delusions/psychosis?

Existential psychotherapy is quite sceptical of over-structured forms of diagnosis. Psychosis is a changeable syndrome, often defined by the existence of delusions and hallucinations. Despite tremendous work, the essence of psychosis is still elusive and, though some theories were adopted by different researchers, few would assert that the aetiology of psychosis is known (van Os et al., 2009). Thus, the usefulness of their concept has been repeatedly questioned and the variability and nature of symptoms and their impact on diagnoses are often a cause of confusion to psychiatrists. Delusions are frequently present in individuals suffering from mood disorder (Winters & Neal, 1983) and are present among manic individuals. They are even found in those suffering from depression. Hallucinations are also present in various conditions and should not be considered as pathognomonic for psychosis diagnosis. The 1960s produced many critics of conventional psychiatric practice such as Szasz (1961) and Laing (1960) who negated the legitimacy of the mental disease model in general and with regard to schizophrenia and psychosis in particular. They both criticised the biological direction for explaining emotional distress, arguing that no biological factor has been identified that would explain the behaviour of patients. Instead, they concentrated on contextual connections within a distressed person's behaviour, his family, and personal history. These critiques attracted a fair amount of attention from the general public at the time but did not have a significant impact in psychiatric circles, although their experimental clinics opened up a rich vein of discussion.

The dominant medical intervention has to be seen, despite its potentially detrimental effects, as necessary in some situations. It should be regarded as a temporary first-aid strategy only; as it is not a holistic model of analysing and understanding human nature. This emphasises the flaws of the medical model as a sole perspective for distresses of the soul, rather than arguing in favour of an overall ban of the use of drugs in acute and dangerous situations. These should be used very circumspectly when other avenues have been exhausted and are time limited until it is possible to re-establish communication with the patients.

Phenomenological alternatives when dealing with psychosis and hallucinations allow the investigating therapist to move beyond the assumption that an individual response is in some way not 'normal,' and instead seek to explore the meanings that those responses are expressing (Spinelli, 2011). Furthermore, the potential success of the dialogue depends on the therapist's ability to recognise what is understandable from that which was initially experienced by the client and what is not understandable. In that framework the dialogue would concentrate on what the person is actually experiencing.

In parallel, the therapist would explore how the lived experience is infused with meanings related to the client's life experience. This simultaneous process allows the client to clarify and evaluate his/her experience, while the therapist is able to assist the client by reflecting back this experience and challenging them. That process is possible, as long as it reflects the values and the contradictions that are embedded in the personal meanings given to that experience. Moreover, only when the therapist has demonstrated that they are ready to accept the client's way of being does it becomes possible to restructure a hypothesis that places the client's experience into a broader theoretical framework (Spinelli, 2011). This combination of practical and theoretical enterprise is possible only if the practitioner adopts an unbiased stance that enables him to understand the client's inner world through his clarifications. This will encompass the way the client conceptualises his expressed views and behaviour and so reveal his whole way of being. Furthermore, when these experiences do cause suffering, the real care and support we can extend consists in helping the sufferers meet their needs within the framework of their own subjective experience, rather than trying to bring the experience back into position with objective and acceptable reality (Romme et al., 2009).

Williams (2012) argued that the individual labelled 'psychotic' is entangled in a struggle with the similar core of existential dilemmas with which we all struggle. This reasoning points to the likelihood of psychosis or any kind of hallucinations is not the result of an illness of the brain, but more likely the expression of a mind entrapped in the essential predicaments of existence (ibid.).

In the *Divided Self* (1960), Laing proposed a radical conceptualisation of psychosis. For Laing a person is ontologically secure when they are fully anchored in the reality of the world in which they live, they experience themselves as a whole, and in a temporal sense a continuous person. This person can live in a world with others that he experiences as equal, alive, and whole and has a clear sense of self. However, the ontological insecure individual is unable to meet the world. Everyday circumstances are experienced as a continuous assault and deadly threat; the threat of non-being. Furthermore, the necessity to preserve a stable and safe sense of self when the organisation of one's being is temporary and groundless can prove to be challenging at any time to anyone and even more so in circumstances when the sense of self becomes more fragile. Therefore, it is possible to say that the onset of the state of psychosis is related to the unsustainability of the experience of being in a world where interpersonal conflict cannot be resolved using ordinary strategies (Hoffman, 2005). It is the result of a desperate stratagem when the psyche commences a psychotic process leading to an internal implosion and to a deep and fundamental disintegration; but this is not an irreversible process. The right therapeutic and supportive environment can reverse that trend, reintegrate an eventually re-constructed self that is different from that which existed before the psychotic episode (Calton et al., 2008).

The existential view encompasses moral, human, and philosophical values in its way of approaching the distressed person. This approach has not only a sustainable philosophical basis but has also been proven to deliver a practical viable alternative to the medical model. After re-establishing communication with the patient, the investigation can evolve into an explorative psychotherapy to allow the person to transcend that crisis and decide how to move on to the next step. Masking the symptoms with medications alone, without addressing the fundamental reasons that have caused the psychological implosion, will condemn the client to a drug-deadened existence and will promote the avoidance of responsibility combined with a sense of hopelessness. A flexible, open-minded attitude should be maintained, to benefit clients with a broad and inclusive focus that will transcend traditional diagnostic barriers, keeping the respect and dignity of the client intact.

4.8   How do existential therapists work with suicidal clients?

The phenomenon of suicide is one of the main concerns for every mental health practitioner in general and existential therapists in particular, in so far as it raises fundamental existential issues relating to the meaning of life; freedom of choice and respecting the choice of others. It also highlights the existential therapists' commitment to stand shoulder to shoulder with our human fellows in times of crisis, with the paradoxes and internal conflicts these may create.

The limited aspects of life, its *thrownness* and uncertainty regarding everything bar the certainty of death, holds an inherent element of absurdity, which raises questions concerning life's purpose. Existential philosophers have pondered upon the meaning of life, the lack of it, and the absurdity of life in different ways (see Section 1.4). However, the philosopher most identified with the notion of the Absurd was Albert Camus (2000).

Camus proposed that in order to investigate and understand the phenomena of suicide, one should investigate the message behind this act. What does it communicate to us? What does it imply? In doing so, he suggests that those who consider, attempt, or commit suicide are making a statement about their relationship with life. He further argues that this statement amounts to a confession that life is too much and not worth the trouble. Thus, Camus suggests a new way of conceptualising suicide not as a result of an event or a contributing factor but rather as a judgment on the value of life, or the result of a crisis in which the value of life is questioned (Roberts & Lamont, 2014); concluding that life does not hold enough worth, and therefore in accordance with that conclusion is not worth living.

The absurd is to be comprehended as a clash, a frustrating contradiction between the profound human quest for life to have a meaning, a higher purpose or grand explanation that provides a context within which the struggles and difficulties in a person's life can make sense – and the realisation that unfortunately there is no such context or, if there is, it is beyond our scope of comprehension (Camus, 2000).

This clash between the personal quest for meaning and the fact that there is no inherent meaning built into life is seen as a split separating the Self and its quest for oneness. A clash between seeking unity in the fragmented universe in which we operate and above all in the contradictions that hold it together (ibid.).

Framing suicide through the existential philosophy lens proposes a different understanding of this phenomenon. It separates suicide from being automatically identified as the result of mental illness and conceptualises it as an attempt to address an existential issue; the issue that is located at the very heart of human existence. It becomes a challenging enterprise to make sense of the struggles and difficulties of life.

This radical approach to suicide is challenging the orthodox model which views suicide as the result of mental health issues, with its heavy reliance upon medications and hospitalisation. Instead, an existential approach relates it to the individual experiencing an existential crisis created by their confrontation with the absurd aspects of life, without the possibility to create meaning or as a result of unbearable suffering originating from intensely difficult physical, mental, and emotional experiences. It is the combination of physical, mental, and emotional dimensions that transform suffering to unbearable suffering. Unbearable suffering can only be comprehended and recognised as the sufferers' perspective of time of the past, the present, and expectations (or lack of it) of the future. Thus, hopelessness is described as a dominant aspect of unbearable suffering (Dees et al., 2011).

The therapist will endeavour to forge a relationship with the individual and create a space in which their loss of meaning is being held, it will include validating the individual's experience, and offering a space in which they can explore their subjective experiences without pathologising them. In that space the client is encouraged to express their loss of meaning side by side with exploring their values, past and present, and to be able to engage in an authentic and meaningful dialogue in response to the profoundly challenging existential aspects of suicide. Truly brave exploration and a re-evaluation of values and old beliefs and their social and perhaps cultural context would provide an opportunity for expanding their sense of self and by doing so encourage them to create new meanings and a sense of a possible future.

4.9　How do therapists work with chronic pain from an existential approach?

Pain is one of the most common causes of human suffering. It is an integral part of life which can be seen as an alarm signal for a failure of the functioning body but equally a nuisance that needs to be removed. Yet despite recognising its value as a protective measure, most people find it unbearable and will struggle with making sense of it, which makes their suffering more difficult to bear.

Medically, pain is often viewed as the result of a problem created by a disease or by a specifically stricken part of the body, but this ignores the individual subjective experience of the pain or being with pain. This view stems from the biomedical model which conceptualises humans as compartmentalised beings. This perception of pain as a localised and disconnected phenomenon reflects the western Cartesian duality of the separation between body and mind and is based on a positivist view of reality; the existence of one objective reality which ignores the subjective experience of that reality, or in this context that subjective levels of pain cannot be empirically proven. Privately ignoring physical pain may be particularly strong in societies which value stoicism. However, limiting the perception of pain to its sensory physical response does not address the phenomenon of chronic pain .in all its complexity.

Chronic pain phenomenon is a multi-dimensional experience involving physical, psychological, and social factors, and therefore needs to be addressed as a subjective experience inseparable from the person suffering from it. Existential therapy holds a holistic view of the individual which views humans as *beings* whose interaction with the world is co-created between the external and internal reality in which they live and that the body, mind, and the world in which they live are interconnected and contribute to the existence of each other (ibid.). An existential perspective therefore provides an understanding that living with chronic pain affects the whole person's existence on all four dimensions (Deurzen, 2012) and as such impacts and shapes the pain and the way it is experienced by the client.

The experience of chronic pain can be very isolating if it is difficult to communicate and share. This state may amplify the sense of helplessness. As a result, the client will find themselves adding layers of suffering in addition to the original pain. The therapeutic space will allow the client to be seen and heard by their existential therapist, since the latter will focus on holding a space for the client to allow them to describe their experience as they experience it.

After the creation of that holding space, the exploration will expand into meaning making of the client's experience. Every experience is understood and catalogued by each individual based on the meaning ascribed to it. Exploring the meaning of the experience and exploring different possible meanings will be the starting point of the work undertaken by both therapist and client. Meaning making of that experience for the client is based on their lived experience, their understanding of it, and the meaning they make of their lives so far. The meaning in life is a subjective construct and is created by every one of us according to our ideals, values, and expectations. This constitutes the basis upon which we make our choices and create our own life. Thus, the existential therapist will assist their clients in exploring their views about their life in general and their lives with the pain in particular. Revisiting these values and expectations will open a vast terrain of exploration and perhaps a re-calibration of the world view of the client. Understanding how the pain is experienced and its correlation to the set of values and expectations they hold will help them understand the experience and perhaps reshape it according to newfound values or expectations that are longer relevant to the life that they live.

According to Frankl (2014) suffering is an integral and unavoidable part of life, whether it includes physical pain or not and enduring it requires finding meaning in the suffering. Suffering stripped of meaning will continue to increase the suffering since it is experienced as meaningless and amounts to nothing. Frankl argued that the search for meaning in itself allows agency and thus encourages the person to take responsibility for their own choices. These choices will include the way they choose to relate to the pain and therefore the way they will experience their consequent suffering. The creation of meaning for a client suffering from chronic pain and understanding the permanence of the pain requires meaning. When the choice of opting out is no longer available, the only alternative is for change to occur inwardly; thus, transforming suffering into realisation and accepting the limited aspects of life. By doing so the client will become aware of the choices available to them.

Each person is unique and should be regarded as such. This means that a one-size-fits-all approach will never be the answer to personalised suffering. Creating the space for the client to be seen and share their experiences with an attentive therapist who meets the client without an agenda, and who explores the client's world views and creates the possibility for a shift in their world view, will allow the client to find new meanings in that difficult experience and choose to relate to it accordingly.

4.10   Do existential therapists work with couples and families?

Existential family and couple therapy broadly focuses on the ability of the couple or of different family members to address the existential dimensions of their problems. In particular the work will inevitably focus on the social dimension of existence and the tension created within that dimension between togetherness and isolation. Similar to individual therapy, there is no set manual or techniques to address these problems. It is, rather, a process of learning about the self and their relationships with others and the tension that is created from the juxtaposition of both processes. It aims to explore the concept of togetherness and separateness. The aim of the therapy is to create an open and honest dialogue that will help the participants to make their choices in regard to their particular family unit or partnership.

The existential givens include the interplay between an individual's personal freedom and their awareness of their freedom of choice, coupled with their sense of responsibility toward themselves and the couple or the family they are forming. This also implies accepting that anxiety is an inherent part of human relationships and with it, the inescapability of avoiding conflicts. Each active participant in this therapy will need to access their courage to confront and recognise their own perceptions, biases, and feelings as well as these in others, and this will require flexibility and creativity. The aim of this approach is to challenge the limitations of life whilst being able to recognise the freedom of choice we have within these limitations.

Although there are no set ways of working existentially with families and couples, there are common concepts that inform the work of the existential therapist.

As in individual therapy the approach is phenomenological, which means that it concentrates on the lived experience of each individual in the unit; their lived experience of themselves as individuals and their lived experience as being part of that unit. This phenomenological approach enables the therapist to stay present with their clients to help them to gain a better sense of their own preconceptions and biases. This is particularly useful as it allows each person in the room the space to explore and voice their own lived experience of separateness and togetherness and gives the opportunity for each member of the unit to witness what it means to be the other.

Existentially we exist in relation to others. Existential philosophers such as Heidegger and Buber, Nietzsche, and Kierkegaard have argued that individuality is secondary to relationships (Deurzen & Iacovou, 2013). We start our lives with others and as part of others and we gradually learn to master our individuality and negotiate, more or less successfully, that conundrum. We cannot be fully separated from others, even when alone, our mind is still inhabited with the presence of others. This means that the challenge of togetherness is indeed seen as part of human existence that will define us and our vision of ourselves. This premise is at the basis of the philosophical approach to couple and family therapy and will inform the approach to therapy.

The dialogical space between humans is often messy and unruly, which can obscure the views and the feelings of the individual members of the family or the couple. Therefore, part of the work will be to encourage all participants to be open when taking part in the dialogue whilst remembering that they occupy a shared space within the unit. This does not necessarily imply compromise, but about recognising the meeting points upon which they may build understanding. This allows time to listen to each other and discover how it feels to be the other.

Humans need meaning; we need to make sense of what is happening to us and around us in order to process it. Therefore, existential therapy holds a view that families or couples can change their perception and attitude towards the reality of their social situation when members of the unit are able to find a meaning and purpose for change (Lantz, 2004). Furthermore, existential therapy will invariably involve expanding the awareness of the different meanings each member ascribes to, such as a certain value or certain experience and the contextual aspect of it. Each individual organises their perspective of reality according to their views, which may differ when they are on their own or when they are part of a unit. This entails understanding and acknowledging what each member of the unit values and clarifying it, so that everyone has a clear understanding of what matters to each one, which is not based on assumptions.

The aim of existential therapy in this context is to help clients understand the tension between togetherness and separateness as is manifested in the dialogue. It is about expanding awareness of the disadvantages of polarising separateness and togetherness rather than learning to hold them together as part of the human existence and thus allowing the beginning of a real dialogue. It recognises that this is a dynamic process which will always be a work in progress for a couple or for all members of the family and that they must accept and learn to work with this ongoing tension.

Further reading

Deurzen, E. van (2012). *Existential Counselling & Psychotherapy in Practice*. Sage Publications.

Deurzen, E. van, & Arnold-Baker, C. (2018). *Existential Therapy: Distinctive Features*. Routledge.

Frankl, V. (2014). *A Man in Search of Meaning*. Simon and Shuster.

Stolorow, R. (2007). *Trauma and Human Existence: Autobiographical, Psychoanalytic, and Philosophical Reflections*. Routledge.

Yalom, I. (2002). *The Gift of Therapy*. Piatkus Books.

References

Boss, M. (1983). *The Existential Foundations of Medicine and Psychology*. Jason Aronson.

Calton, T., Ferriter, M., Huband, N., & Spandler, H. (2008). A Systematic Review of the Soteria Paradigm for the Treatment of People Diagnosed With Schizophrenia, *Schizophrenia Bulletin, 34*, 181–92. https://doi.org/10.1093/schbul/sbm047

Campos-Winter, H. (2020). Being itself, limit situation, temporality and existence as an analytical structure for existential enlightenment. *Open Journal of Philosophy, 10*, 113–128.

Camus, A. (2000). *The Myth of Sisyphus*. Penguin.

Carreno, D.F., & Pérez-Escobar (please keep the name as is), J.A. (2019). Addiction in existential positive psychology (EPP, PP2.0): From a critique of the brain disease model towards a meaning-centered approach. *Counselling Psychology Quarterly*, *32*(3–4), 415–435.

Dees, M.K., Vernooij-Dassen, M.J., Dekkers, W.J., et al. (2011). 'Unbearable suffering': A qualitative study on the perspectives of patients who request assistance in dying. *Journal of Medical Ethics*, *37*, 727–734.

Deurzen, E. van (2012). *Existential Counselling & Psychotherapy in Practice*. Sage Publications.

Deurzen, E. van (2023). Existential therapy for grief. In N. Steffen, E. Milman, & R. A. Neimeyer (Eds.). *The Handbook of Grief Therapies*. Sage, 69–77.

Deurzen, E. van, & Iacovou, S. (2013). *Existential Perspectives on Relationship Therapy*. Bloomsberry Publishing.

DuBose, T. (2010). Trauma. In D.A. Leeming, K. Madden, & S. Marlan (Eds.), *Encyclopaedia of Psychology and Religion*. Springer, 925–928.

Du Plexis, G. (2018). An existential perspective on addiction treatment: A logic-based therapy case study. *International Journal of Philosophical Practice*, *5*(1), 1–32.

Felder, A.J., & Robbins, B.D. (2021). Approaching mindful multicultural case formulation: Rogers, Yalom and existential phenomenology. *Person-Centered & Experiential Psychotherapies*, *20*(1), 1–20.

Frankl, V. (2014). *A Man in Search of Meaning*. Simon and Shuster.

Freud, S. (1957). Mourning and melancholia. In J. Strachey (ed. & trans.). *The Complete Psychological Works of Sigmund Freud* (vol. 14). Hogarth (originally published 1917), 243–258.

Greening, T. (1992). Existential challenges and responses. *The Humanistic Psychologist*, *20*, 1–6.

Heidegger, M. (1996). *Being and Time*. Sunny.

Hoffman, L. (2005). *Existential Perspectives on Diagnosis*. Retrieved on 11 June 2015, from: www.existential-therapy.com/existential_ topics/Diagnosis.htm

Hoffman, L., & Cleare-Hoffman, H.P. (2017). An existential-humanistic approach to case formulation and treatment planning.

Poster presented at the 125th Annual Convention of the American Psychological Association, Washington, DC.

Jaspers, K. (1970). *Philosophy, volume II*. (E. B. Ashton, trans.). The University of Chicago Press.

Kierkegaard, S. (2014). *The Concept of Anxiety*. (A. Hannay, trans.). Liverlight.

Klass, D., & Stephan, E.M. (2018). *Continuing Bonds in Bereavement: New Directions for Research and Practice*. Routledge.

Laing, R.D. (1960). *The Divided Self: An Existential Study in Sanity and Madness*. Tavistock Publications Ltd.

Lantz, J. (2004). World view concepts in existential family therapy. *Contemporary Family Therapy, 26*, 165–178.

Levine, P., & Frederick, A. (1997). *Waking the Tiger: Healing Trauma through the Innate Capacity to Transform Overwhelming Experiences*. North Atlantic Books.

Lima, D.D., Alves, V.L., & Turato, E.R. (2014). The phenomenological-existential comprehension of chronic pain: Going beyond the standing healthcare models. *Philosophy, Ethics, and Humanities in Medicine, 9*(2). https://doi.org/10.1186/1747-5341-9-2

Madison, G. (2005). Bereavement and loss. In E. van Deurzen & C. Arnold-Baker (Eds.), *Existential Perspectives on Human Issues, a Handbook for Therapeutic Practice*. Palgrave-MacMillan, 197–206.

May, R. (2015). *The Meaning of Anxiety*. W. W. Norton & Co.

Roberts, M., & Lamont, E. (2014). Suicide: An existentialist reconceptualization. *Psychiatric and Mental Health Nursing, 21*(10), 873–878.

Romme, M., Escher, S., Dillon, J., & Corstens, D. (2009). *Living with Voices: 50 Stories of Recovery*. PCCS Books.

Sartre, J-P. (1966). *Being and Nothingness: An Essay on Phenomenological Ontology*. Washington Square Press.

Spinelli, E. (2011). *Psychosis: New Existential, Systemic and Cognitive Behavioral Developments*. Retrieved on 15 July 2015, from: http://media.proquest.com.ezproxy.mdx.ac.uk/media/pq/classic/doc/386233431/fmt/ai/rep/

Stolorow, R. (2007). *Trauma and Human Existence: Autobiographical, Psychoanalytic, and Philosophical Reflections*. Routledge.

Szasz, T. (1961). *The Myth of Mental Illness: Foundations of a Theory of Personal Conduct*. Hoeber-Harper,

Temple, M., & Gall, T.L. (2018). Working through existential anxiety toward authenticity: A spiritual journey of meaning making. *Journal of Humanistic Psychology*, *58*(2), 168–193.

van Os, J., Linscott, R.J., Myin-Germeys, I., Delespaul, P., & Krabbendam, L. (2009). A systematic review and meta-analysis of the psychosis continuum: Evidence for a psychosis proneness-persistence-impairment model of psychotic disorder. *Psychological Medicine*, *39*(2), 179–195.

Wiklund, L. (2008). Existential aspects of living with addiction – Part II: Caring needs. A hermeneutic expansion of qualitative findings. *Journal of Clinical Nursing*, *17*(18), 2435–2443.

Williams, P. (2012). *Brain Disease or Existential Crisis? – Mad in America*. Retrieved on 4 August 2015, from: www.madinamerica.com/2012/08/op-ed-schizophreniapsychosis-brain-disease-or-existential-crisis/

Winters, K.C., & Neal J.M. (1983). Delusions and delusional thinking in psychotics: A review of the literature. *Clinical Psychology Review*, *3*, 227–253.

Wong, P.T. (2010). Meaning therapy: An integrative and positive existential psychotherapy. *Journal of Contemporary Psychotherapy*, *40*(2), 85–93.

Yalom, I.D. (1980). *Existential Psychotherapy*. Basic Books.

Part 5

Existential relevance to everyday life

Questions about the application of existential ideas to ordinary everyday living

Simon Wharne

5.1 How can we be free when life is full of duties, chores, and obstacles?

Although many different philosophical positions are found within existentialism, there are broad over-arching themes. The tension between freedom and responsibility is one of these themes. Søren Kierkegaard wrote his student thesis on Socratic irony (Kierkegaard, 1912a). He found with Socrates a shared sense of paradox in the human experience of freedom. Socrates lived in Athens at a time when the state was experimenting with a form of democracy. The people were no longer subjected to the will of a tyrant, and they expected to enjoy more freedom. An irony can be found, therefore, in the reality that citizens were required to take their turn in serving the community. They took on judicial and administrative roles, maintaining order, and curtailing their own freedoms.

Socrates had asked the question: 'how should we live?' and this question caused a lot of trouble. In his way of debating, Socrates would reveal the limited nature of human knowledge. This undermined common assumptions, including the religious doctrines that everyone else upheld. His ironic form of questioning will establish the absence of any certainty or foundation for the choices we make (this questioning is explored in Section 2.7). Inspired by Socrates, Kierkegaard took a critical stance

DOI: 10.4324/9781003355700-6

in relation to the religious practices of his time, in nineteenth-century Denmark (1912b, p. 368). He observed how people were choosing to follow expected moral standards of behaviour, mainly because they would gain thereby in social standing, and they would prosper.

Following Socrates, Kierkegaard did not claim to know the truth. He published under different pseudonyms, using irony to argue from conflicting perspectives. Like Socrates, he was challenging assumptions. He was trying to get his readers to realise their freedoms, to take responsibility for their choices, not just to follow the crowd. For example, he questioned the possibility that we can be certain of the existence of God. He suggested instead that a belief of this nature could only be founded on faith (Kierkegaard, 1912c). We are free therefore to adopt this faith, but we retain our responsibility for making that choice. This means that we cannot delegate our choices to a higher power. In the absence of certainty, people would have no reason to slavishly follow any practices religious or secular. It is not enough, for example, to follow the ethical codes of a professional body without certainty, we must make our own choices every moment, in each new unfolding dilemma.

How then should we live, if there is no universal guidance by which to anticipate or solve the challenging dilemmas we face? Again, how do we choose if our being has no essence or consistency? If, as Jean-Paul Sartre claimed, our freedom to decide today is not impeded by what has happened in our past (1943). We might rationalise and justify when we have already chosen. We might explain our choice as an outcome of our character, or the result of some process of subconscious or social cause and effect. No, it is the other way around! We find out about ourselves, and get to have a character, only when we make choices in the flow of events. It is in our deciding that the nature of our being is brought into fruition (Eger, 2017).

Martin Heidegger wrote about the way that we are thrown into being, in the unique life that we are living (1927). He observed the facticity of that being, in the sense that we did not choose the time or place of our birth, the form of our given embodiment, or our culture. Perhaps for you, it does not feel as if you choose to be caught in the mundane duties and chores of your everyday existence. In relation to Socrates' question of 'how should we live?,' Heidegger asks you to consider what would be a free and authentic response to where it is that you find yourself. Victor Frankl extended this thinking. He made the challenging claim that, even when all other freedoms are taken from us, we are still free to choose the stance that we take (Frankl, 1946).

Our freedom is contingent and constrained by the nature of time. There are some choices that will never be open for us, or if they are, we only get them once and we cannot go back to remake them. Edith Stein used the example of the creative and artistic person, observing that their talent might not be expressed, or it might go unnoticed (1922). It is only when others take interest that we find opportunities for self-expression, and our gifts unfold. Our genius is brought into being only if that door opens for us, and we choose to step through it. Yet even if we do not get the opportunities we seek, we are still free to choose the stance we take towards that.

Karl Jaspers describes 'boundary situations' in which we come up against our existence, and if we do find the freedom to move on, it is only ever into another limited life situation (1932, p. 178). Irvin Yalom provides a similar account in his description of existential givens (1980). We all have our unique lives to live, but we will all die. We will all encounter other people. We are all embodied. We must all establish our own sense of meaning and purpose. Yet, once more, it is only by making choices that we can hold that meaning and purpose. This is the irony of freedom. Whenever we make a commitment to a choice, we give up on the multitude of alternatives that we could have chosen. We have taken a step towards our arrival in our own chosen being, but are we getting the irony of our situation? We do not know how future events will unfold, or the meanings that will be attached to the choices we made.

5.2   Can people ever truly love each other, or are they always more selfish than caring?

As a student Martin Heidegger was a part of the academic circle that formed around Edmund Husserl. This was a network of bright thinkers, exploring new ideas. It must have seemed that life was opening, with intense conversations, in the forging of meaningful relationships. Then, the Nazis introduced racist and antisemitic policies. In response to this, Heidegger was more selfish than caring. He found opportunities to advance his career (Bakewell, 2017). Divisions set in, and the construction of otherness has become another important theme in existential writings.

Edith Stein studied under Husserl and became his assistant (Bakewell, 2017). They were both born into Jewish families. Then, as a woman, Stein met unbreachable barriers when trying to advance her career. Due to antisemitic policies, Husserl was banned from using the university library. He resigned from his post as rector. Heidegger had replaced Stein as Husserl's assistant, and he then replaced Husserl as rector of the university. Stein, who had converted to Catholicism, joined the Carmelite religious order as a nun. She did not choose to leave Europe, as others in her family did. It seems that she accepted her death in a concentration camp. In her love for others, she expressed solidarity in a shared suffering. In her student thesis she addressed the phenomenon of empathy (Stein, 1921) (explored in Section 3.3). In her philosophy, she asked questions of how we relate emotionally to each other, the nature of society, and what it means to be in a community (Stein, 1950, p. 1922).

In 1933, Jean-Paul Sartre was visiting Germany, studying the work of Husserl (Bakewell, 2017). In his own philosophical explorations, Sartre promoted an understanding of human existence in which our selfishness is clearly revealed, claiming that conflict is unavoidable in relationships. Sartre and Simone de Beauvoir debated the idea that we can only alternate between states of being held under that gaze of another, and states of holding the other person in our gaze (Sartre, 1943). They drew this idea from the philosophy of Hegel. Beauvoir did not entirely agree with Sartre, although she did describe the lived experience of being a woman, in a society that is built around the way that men see things (Beauvoir, 1949). She did agree that even when a person is desired, that longing gaze can still turn them into an object, robbing them of their personhood.

Simone de Beauvoir and Jean-Paul Sartre contracted to enjoy an open relationship. They retained their freedom to be intimate with others, while staying devotedly faithful in sharing their academic writings; they commented on, and edited each other's work (Bakewell, 2017). They debated the nature of desire, a state in which we crave that intimacy with the unknown other, only to lose interest in that person when we have possessed them. When we have objectified them, that is, and they have lost their power to hold us in their thrall. Beauvoir and Sartre had sexual encounters with their young students, in a manner that would be seen today as abusive (Seymour-Jones, 2009). We can criticise them now, with hindsight, but we are still objectifying others in ways that these thinkers bought to light. We can even objectify ourselves in the profiling questions of a dating app. We will then be matched with those with whom we are compatible. If we fall in love, perhaps we are only loving an imagined mirror image of ourselves. If we encounter significant hardships and challenges, will our selfishness re-emerge?

When we are selfish and our relationships fail, there are many ways to objectify ourselves, and others. We might meet the criteria for one of the many mental disorders that our clinicians are identifying. When that is, we are too needy, too obsessive, too controlling, too dependent. Perhaps we fit the profile of a narcissist or a psychopath. Love, in this objectification, becomes a form of pathology. Why is it that we cannot just give our partner their space, or let them be themselves? Yet how can we know the person we love, when they have no essence, when as Sartre observed, they might change on a whim, or grow into a different way of being? We thought we knew them, but suddenly they seem quite strange in their otherness (otherness, or 'difference' is reviewed in Section 3.7).

Otherness is a phenomenon that extends beyond gender into ethnicity, religious belief, states of disability, neurodiversity, sexuality, social class, and many more aspects of being. Franz Fanon, wrote, for example, about the experience of always feeling like you are being watched, as a black person, in a world that is viewed from a white perspective (1967). Albert Camus' novel, *The Stranger* (1942) addresses the sense of the absurd, in our encounters with racial and cultural otherness. In response to these debates, Steve Biko placed emphasis on the need to embrace responsibilities and raise consciousness (1978). Contemporary writings, in areas such as neurodiversity and Queer Theory, do not usually get labelled as existential. However, they are extending this tradition of exploring what it means to be other, taking ownership of a way of being. When someone is other, and essentially unknown, it is difficult to love them. In becoming known to themselves, a person makes themselves available for others.

Is it possible then to know each other in the fullness of our being, as Martin Buber (1937) claims? He famously refers to this as an I-thou encounter, rather than an I-it relationship. There are similarities in his reasoning with Stein's account of empathy (1921). Stein observes different stages in the unfolding of empathy. If we open our awareness, we might establish that which is of the other, alongside that which is to do with our self. Empathy in this sense has a temporal quality, as people exist for a moment together between their past and their future. She observes that through 'reiterated empathy' we might gain a better understanding of our self, as seen through the eyes of the other (Stein, 1921).

5.3 Is authenticity about being selfish and doing what we want?

Edith Stein offered a supportive critique of Martin Heidegger's notion of authenticity (Stein, 1950). She was concerned that in what he is saying, he comes close to claiming that community life is always deteriorated, and that authentic being always means lonely being. She asserts that both solitary and community life have their authentic and deteriorated forms (Stein, 1950, p. 81). Stein and Heidegger were both influenced by a phenomenological understanding of time. They considered how we are always becoming, and Heidegger wrote about our orientation to past and future in a present moment (Deurzen & Arnold-Baker, 2018). In this sense, an authentic self is a momentary possibility that we seek to attain, rather than a given state of being. It is a moment that can pass us by, and the Nazi movement which Heidegger joined certainly appears to have been a deteriorated form of community. Perhaps, in that moment in time, Heidegger's opportunity for authenticity passed him by.

Heidegger claimed that Western philosophy had taken the wrong turn in a search for universal and eternal truths (1927). By attending instead to our being and our phenomenological experience in our current duration of time, he sets the notions of God and eternity aside (Orr, 2014). Yet there is still a moral and evangelical quality to what he is saying. Like Søren Kierkegaard, he is critical of those who unthinkingly follow common expectations in their beliefs and actions. He is borrowing from Christian philosophies, when he describes this 'unthinking fitting in' as a state of being fallen. Like Socrates, he is suggesting that the unexamined life is not worth living. This sense in which our purpose and the value of our being are always in question is an existential theme.

In our consumerist cultures, we are constantly driven to enhance our status, to become a successful self. While at the same time our selfish desire to possess reveals a longing for acceptance, as we compete to fit in with the latest trend. Paradoxically, it is this desire for self-expression and popularity that pushes us into conformity. Was Heidegger trying to fit in with the popular crowd when he wore the Nazi insignia? By giving his allegiance to that racist movement, he certainly gained more status and influence. Was he then more able to be his authentic self, because of the freedoms he gained, in his ability to exercise power over others? He claimed that, when confronted by the reality of our own personal death, we will be shocked into living a more authentic manner (Heidegger, 1927). In his view, our death will be highly individual. We are taking that final step out of our existence, he argued, entirely on our own. When we consider this, he would suggest, we realise that we only have this one life. We will work harder therefore to make the most of it.

Is authenticity selfish then, when we take opportunities to do what we want, dominating and disregarding other people? It is thought that, in more collectivist societies, authenticity can be expressed in a relational manner (Wang, 2015). We can truly be ourselves when we experience our existence through closer bonds and commitments to others. However, again, there is no given right way to be. We might assume that, by setting aside our freedoms and always being there for our family and friends, their love and support will always be there for us. That is a selfish assumption. Robert Stolorow observes that traumas, such as bereavement, can shock us out of our complacency just as much as an awareness of our own mortality. Indeed, it is often these traumatic losses that make our shared mortality much more salient for us (Stolorow, 2007).

It is curious, how Heidegger found himself on the wrong side. The wrong side that is as viewed with hindsight, with an awareness that we now have of the atrocities that were committed.

This is strange, when in his philosophical work he is asking us to take a more authentic and moral position. He rejected the philosophy of Edmund Husserl, who was mainly trying to improve the rigor and accuracy of scientific investigation. Edith Stein built on Husserl's approach, exploring the role of empathy in our interpersonal and communal lives. Heidegger tried instead to stand with Socrates and Kierkegaard, asking questions about the right way to live.

Edmund Husserl was seeking ways to observe phenomena, in which our perception is not tainted by our assumptions and everyday thinking. Heidegger rebelled and stood against him, observing that our perceptions of a phenomenon are never separate from what it means to us as people taken up with the concerns of our lives (1927) (this is explored in Section 2.3). However, if we attend to the way that people are responding to their existence, our phenomenological enquiries can reveal aspects of authenticity. We can observe the phenomenon of post-traumatic growth, for example, in which people attain a more authentic way of living. When they accept that trauma and death can happen at any moment, a truth that many of us would prefer not to be reminded of. It is found that people who have come to terms with these realities place more value on being with friends and family. They describe themselves as having developed compassion, wisdom, personal strength, and gratitude, possibly associated with an acceptance of their vulnerabilities and limitations. They appreciate each new day, being less materialistic, more able to live in the present (Joseph, 2012; Tedeschi et al., 1998).

5.4 What is healthy/unhealthy living from an existential perspective?

Emmy van Deurzen has described how we must work in life to maintain our balance (2010). She reminds us that we have an emotional compass, and that this is a guide for us to follow in our response to what happens for us. She observes the four worlds of embodiment, personal psychology, social connectedness, and spirituality (see Section 2.8). While we are living fully in these different worlds, in a balanced manner, we can follow the flow of our emotional awareness.

There are times when we might lose our balance. When we experience trauma, for example, or when we have an illness. This can then have an impact on our social world, if we do not want to attract attention or make a fuss, and others do not then accommodate our distressed and disabled condition. Feeling isolated, we might feel angry and frustrated, asking why did this to happen to me? Our spiritual world is then also no longer in a state of harmony. It can feel as if we are thrown out of the routines that bind us into a shared sense of being in the present with each other (Carel, 2016). We must wait for our body to heal, for our mind to be at peace.

Existential theorists have explored the difficulties we face in our phenomenological experience of lived time. Eugene Minkowski, for example, described how it is that mental health problems can be understood as a failure to experience time in a healthy manner (1933). He corresponded with his colleague Ludwig Binswanger, who also approached mental distress as a disruption in our experience of time (1963). Depression, understood in this framework, is a loss of our orientation towards the future, a loss of balance. The difficulties of the past can press in on the present so that it is impossible to see beyond them. Then in an elated state, we might have a lot of ideas about the future, and we might take on many projects. However, again we are not being in the present to an adequate degree. We neglect to complete all the boring tasks that are necessary to keep our projects on track. When we run around, distracted by every new bright idea, we do not make time to bring any of our exciting possible futures into fruition.

When our thoughts are taken up by that question of how we should live, we might turn to abstract ideas about how our lives ought to be. We might take the view that there is one right way to live and then compare our actual life against that ideal. We forget in this thinking that we cannot step outside of the present moment. Life is not like a journey that has given destinations or staging points. Somethings are predictable, but what happens next in life is largely unknown. While at the same time, because the past is over, it can also seem unfamiliar and strange. Then, being stuck in an expanding present, people can fall into obsessive behaviours. They do not feel able to let the future happen. They repeat compulsive behaviours over and over, trying to reach a state of being ready to move on. This can mean that possible futures do not open for them, when they continue to feel that they cannot let go of their present.

Paul Tillich reminds us that we need courage to live (2014). He observes the benefits we gain in adopting a stoic approach to life. When we take the view that all things will pass. We can decide to calm our emotions, noticing that if we let our feelings rule us, most often we find ourselves driven into chaos and confusion. Tillich also observes the value of living life with passion, in taking opportunities and risks, investing emotionally in our relationships and our ambitions. It is again a matter of balance.

Strangely, everything can seem to be in flux, while at the same time, everything is in suspense. We do not know what will happen, or what people will do. The anxiety that we feel when we are struggling to be present in our current duration of time can be expressed in many ways. Many of us will turn to alcohol and other substances. It can be reassuring and comfortable, to induce that predictable and familiar state of intoxication. Addictions, co-dependence in relationships, over-achieving in work roles, eating disorders, self-harm; they are all spinning out of the urgency with which we seek comfort and certainty. We feel a desperate need to escape the intensity of now. When, that is, all the dreadful things that might happen line up to intrude into our present moment. When all the inadequacies of our past ways of being jostle for our attention.

Existential theorists have been influenced by Eastern philosophies, although not all of them have provided adequate cross-cultural referencing. Kakuzo Okakura gave an account of the cult of tea, as it unfolded in Taoist and Zen philosophies (1906). This exploration is thought to have influenced that circle of phenomenologists who formed around Edmund Husserl. Once more it is the notion of balance which runs through these influential ideas. With our mental health problems, when we are over-anxious, depressed, obsessed, and so on, it is not necessarily the case that there is something wrong with us. It can be argued that most often, these are normal and healthy responses to intolerable life circumstances. While again, these are still situations and responses which we need to bring back into a state of balance. Balance is then another theme that we can observe in existential writings.

5.5   What is the point to life if we are all going to die anyway?

If we are drifting on in the anonymity of the crowd, for a while, we can avoid the prospect of our own death. Martin Heidegger claimed that death is something we face alone, but Edith Stein did not agree. Having taken on a nursing role in the First World War, she spent her time with many wounded and dying soldiers (Macintyre, 2006). She must have been shocked to see so many young men who were traumatised and damaged by the conflict of war. In Robert Stolorow's account of traumatic experiences, he suggests that it is the death of others, as much as our own death, that shocks us out of the everyday flow of normal ways of being (2007).

Stolorow describes how a trauma can take us out of our shared way of relating to time (2007). When that is, part of us longs to go back to being the person we were, before we were abruptly made aware of distressing realities. Suddenly, we are stripped of our familiar distractions and comfortable complacency. We do not know how to move on into the future, and we just want to feel normal again (trauma is considered in Section 4.4). However, in a move towards post-traumatic growth (Joseph, 2012), we might adopt that more authentic way of being, in which we are present with each other and with the truths of existence.

It is uncomfortable to consider the enormity of death, which is a central existential theme. The few years of our existence are less than a blink of the eye in the history of the universe. Many of us throw our energies into projects so that we will live on in the memory of others after our death. We are perhaps seeking a sense of permanence and significance. However, with the passing of time, all records of our existence will be washed away. This can free us to do what we want with our lives, because our lives matter only to ourselves and those we care about now. Is this the reason why we are willing to damage our planet in such a reckless manner? We know of the devastating impact of our choices, in terms of lost habitats and extinct species, while also, it is our own current collective cultural existence that we are risking. Climate change is for us an existential threat.

Socrates took responsibility for the choices he made. He was concerned that if he harmed others, he would damage his own being. He stood against his fellow Greeks, who placed a lot of responsibility in the hands of their gods. They feared that it would be wrong to step away from the path set for them, by their fate (Deurzen, 2010). The stories they told were often cautionary, warning us not to defy the gods, asking us to accept our position and expected future. Should we follow Socrates then, and accept that it is not the gods who are causing climate change; that we must work harder to limit the negative impacts of our existence?

Albert Camus drew on the Greek myth of Sisyphus, a mortal who overstepped the mark and was punished (1955) (as discussed in Section 1.4). Sisyphus was condemned to roll a boulder up a hill every day, just to see it roll down again, so that he must repeat his labour. Camus observes that even in this limited existence, Sisyphus can work with dignity. He has a reason to be. We might feel that our lives lack meaning or purpose, but we can still take pride in our work, every day, as we engage in the apparently fruitless task of seeking our own reason to be.

Life is unpredictable. People are unreliable. Things change, so we might conclude that it is best to withdraw into a passive acceptance. Unfortunately, life can still seek us out and pull us into impossible dilemmas, in which we stand alone facing uncomfortable realities. We might therefore decide to live life to the full, taking risks, rushing into every opportunity that comes up. Alternatively, we can hope that there is a middle path, a way of living that is balanced and healthy.

The ideas that we are exploring here have been debated and clarified by each of the theorists referenced in the text. Each of them dedicated their time to the task of understanding the human condition. Most of them have died, or they will die, and so will we. What is the point then of considering what they have said in their philosophies? Well, we have not died yet, and we live now in a world shaped by their ideas. Our everyday ways of being and relating to others are influenced by the history of our culture's philosophical explorations. Our world today is different from the world that we might have been living in, because of the ideas that these philosophers explored and promoted. If we join in the debate, living with a passionate concern for each other and for our planet, perhaps future generations will inherit a better world.

5.6   Does it matter what meaning system I follow?

When existential theorists are asking that question, 'how should we live?,' they are not necessarily suggesting that there is one or other correct way to be. Usually, they ask this question to reveal the absence of any firm or certain guidance for us to follow. Most would agree that, even if we did find an excellent guide which is full of good advice, we would still need to choose to follow it. For a while perhaps, we can hide behind excuses: 'I was just following orders,' or 'I was just doing what everybody else was doing.' Life tends to pick us out from the crowd, to require that we account for our own choices.

What should we do when we are born into a specific culture, a religious community, or an ethnicity which carries a lot of tradition? When we find ourselves already trying to live in what we believe to be the correct way, long before we are mature enough to consider if this is what we would choose. We face a dilemma, should we cling more closely to our familiar certainties, taking the view that everyone else has got it wrong? Or is there a more authentic response to our unfolding awareness that other people do things differently.

If we consider our history, we can observe that philosophical debates flourish in those times and places where there are lot of cross-cultural encounters. There were trading networks in the ancient world centred around Greece, expanding, and then extending further as the Romans built their empire. Rome was a multicultural mix of ethnicities. Centuries later the Muslim world opened and extended to include varying cultures. Science and philosophy developed as academics translated diverse literature into Arabic. Many cultures met and shared ideas in the trade routes across Asia. Then, northern Europe expanded its influence across the globe. We might assume that these expansions were a form of assimilation, as dominate belief systems were imposed on others. However, our beliefs have changed and developed, influenced by cross-cultural encounters and debates. Religious practices and secular traditions have changed and will change again.

It is when we become aware that there are alternative ways to live, alternative belief systems, that our existential dilemmas come more clearly into focus. We could be concerned by the idea that existential theory has most often been explored by white people in a Western cultural tradition (this is considered in Section 1.2). Alternatively, we can attend to the way these explorations are often conversational, a response to other cultures and ways of being. It is in the more cosmopolitan networks that existential theory has developed. Jean-Paul Sartre found his life disrupted when France was occupied during the Second World War, a difficult cross-cultural encounter (Bakewell, 2017). With his country's liberation, he did not write about the joy of returning to a familiar way of being. He continued with his exploration of the dizziness of freedom.

Wars have raged on since Jean-Paul Sartre observed the open nature of freedom. Refuges and migrants continue to flow between nations. Sartre found himself caught up in debates, positioned in opposition to his friend Albert Camus (Bakewell, 2017). They were assumed to hold different views on the liberation of Algeria, and on French colonialism. Sartre, Simone de Beauvoir, and their network of fellow academics were caught in similar disputes in relation to communism. It is not easy, in these conflicts, to pick out one consistent philosophy, or political position. This was the backdrop to Jacques Derrida's challenging observations on our use of language (1976). At a time when academics and philosophers were obsessively seeking the underlying frameworks and causal processes behind human affairs, Derrida reduced their efforts to little more than a play on words.

Post-modern philosophy developed out of the academic deputes of the late twentieth century. In an increasingly global world, the former monolithic modernist projects of nation states were fading away. Paul Ricoeur wrote about the linguistic turn in social sciences, as existential thought developed (1981). He observes that we cannot go back to ask an author to clarify what they meant. Even if that author is still alive they might not be sure themselves exactly what they were trying to convey through the words they wrote. In reading texts, we can only appropriate their meanings to make sense of things in our world now. The world of the author is in the past and in our efforts to reconstruct that world, we are always interpreting and transforming it, as it comes to be seen through the eyes of our own world.

We have some certainties in the existential givens of life. Time will always have passed and if we are still alive, it is most likely that we will have adapted and changed in the process of getting into the future. There are things we will have lost, and things we will have gained. Whatever meaning system we have adopted in the past, we must remake that choice again today, and every future day. Making meaning is another existential theme.

5.7 Will existential therapy/ideas make me happy?

Maurice Merleau-Ponty observed that emotions are not just internal states. They are partly a form of communication, evident in our disposition, a response to where we find ourselves (Merleau-Ponty, 1945). The way we feel provides an essential guide, in the emotional compass that Emmy van Deurzen describes (2010). We will need this guide if we are to chart our way through difficulties. Jean-Paul Sartre had described how our feelings are orientated towards our future, a means of negotiating in our relationships (1972). There is then a potential for us to choose the emotional stance that we adopt. We can observe the patterns in our ways of relating to others and then decide to do things differently (as discussed in Section 1.3, existentialism is a positive philosophy).

Emotions are sometimes treated therapeutically as if they were purely material. As if they were only an individual physiological state that we passively experience. If we are unhappy, for example, this is then approached as a problem within us. However, we might prefer to stay with our familiar disposition, no matter how limiting that is. We might, for example, fall into the habit of feeling sad, or superficially happy, or cynical, or indifferent (this is a form of sedimentation, as described in Section 2.6). We avoid situations and thinking in which we would experience other emotions. Cognitive Behavioural Therapy (CBT) practitioners might observe how we maintain our misperceptions, by only noticing whatever it is that confirms our thinking and maintains our assumed emotional stance. Thoughts feelings and behaviours are connected, but often, there are good reasons why we would seek the safety and familiarity of our emotional coping strategies.

Even when the people around us just want us to be happy and successful, their expectations can weigh heavy upon us. It is all too easy to fall into a feigned cheerfulness, in which uncomfortable truths are neglected. When no one mentions the elephant in the room, and everyone is dancing around a difficult truth. Perhaps we are colluding with a shared denial because we need to placate someone who holds power over us. Or perhaps we are pulled into toxic positivity because the truth is too painful, and we are trying to protect others who are vulnerable. We can feel that we are under pressure from these others, who insist that we must cheer up, that we adopt a more positive view on life. It can be useful then, when existential theory attends to difficult things like death trauma and meaninglessness. This can help us to prick that superficial bubble.

Some people talk about having good and bad days. A perfect day, they might suggest, is a day when nothing goes wrong. Yet if we are fully experiencing life, we can feel overwhelming joy and devastating distress on the same day. If we are fully engaged in all aspects of existence, we will experience all possible emotional responses. This will be a challenge, but perhaps we can find perfection in that rounded and emotionally complete expansive day. Life is not going to unfold fully for us while we stubbornly continue in our efforts to pick out and experience only our preferred emotional states.

In some therapeutic approaches we are encouraged to rate the severity of our more distressing emotions; often on a scale of nought to five. Existential theory inherits a different philosophy. Immanuel Kant did not believe that emotions come in quantifiable degrees (1786). Also, we are not passively experiencing our emotions. They are part of a stance that we are taking towards where it is that we find ourselves. If, for example, we take the view that people will always let us down, we are not open to the joy of discovering how much they care about us. Or if we always look for the best in people, perhaps we are denying the potential for others to be cruel and destructive. In Edith Stein's account of empathy, she observes that we do not always attend fully to what is happening in our encounters. When we assume that someone has good intentions, in the same way that we have, we are taken in by a fraudster (Stein, 1921, p. 86). Yet, she observes that if we have that stronger sense of good will, the disturbing feelings that invade our being can be repelled.

Emotions, as an existential theme, are always flowing through us and we are always in one mood or another (Heidegger, 1927). When we see a human figure depicted in a work of art, a picture or sculpture, we have an emotional response. We know that there is no real person before us, yet we find ourselves reading emotions into the face that we see looking back at us, and in the bodily stance that we observe. We cannot help but entertain the possibility of consciousness behind the painted eyes. Those eyes might follow us as we move around the room, asking something of us. This reveals the intersubjective emotional nature of our being with others. Even when we are alone, our internal dialogue presents the expectations and pressures of others. We are always anticipating how we will be understood, judged, included, or excluded. There is no escape from these possibilities. To live fully and authentically, we must be open, and we must navigate a way through all these possibilities, along with the emotional responses that we will have to them.

5.8   Is it okay to self-harm or kill myself?

Ludwig Binswanger expressed some challenging thinking when he described suicide as the greatest freedom that we have (1963, p. 258). He took the questionable decision to discharge a patient who was actively suicidal; that patient died by poisoning herself shortly afterwards (Binswanger, 1958). Similarly, Jean-Paul Sartre seems to have considered the possibility of death at our own hands as just another aspect of our radical freedom. He uses a French expression: '*L'Appel du Vide,*' or the call of the void, to describe an intrusive desire to throw oneself over the edge when walking by a cliff (Sartre, 1943). It was Albert Camus, a one-time friend of Sartre, who proposed that the question of whether life is worth living or not should be our most pressing philosophical concern (1955).

It can seem strange that existential philosophers find meaning in this question of whether our lives are worth living or not. In our contemporary societies, if we are ruminating over this question, we might find ourselves being assessed by a psychiatrist. Our concerns could be interpreted as 'suicidal ideation,' a symptom of mental illness. There are zero-tolerance campaigns, whereby a view of suicidality is promoted in which the person is overwhelmed and passive (Campo, 2009). Suicidality is understood to be brought about by depression, or another mental health problem. In this thinking, if a person does try to take their own life, they are relieved of any responsibility for their actions. Blame is shifted onto the healthcare professionals who should have treated the mental illness.

When psychological therapists borrow from medical understandings, they are perhaps diminishing the significance of a person's distress. Those who are seeking political asylum, for example, will sometimes make the statement that they would rather take their own life than face the torture and painful death that would result if they were deported (Blackwell, 2009, p. 115). Some people in this situation have gone on hunger strike. Are they suffering from a mental illness? Do they have an eating disorder? Or, is their protest and their choice to take their life a rational and active expression of their will? It is important in these explorations to not to collude with or condone risky behaviours. We must find a way to understand and accept, without agreeing that it is right for a person to be harming themselves. It is not for us to decide whether someone else's self-harm or suicidality constitute reasonable or sensible choices.

Where there are risks, psychological therapists can be found to be failing in their moral duty if they do not treat a mental health problem. However, they are also failing if they collude with oppressive political policies. If our government policies leave some people impoverished and excluded, state-sponsored psychological therapies might only be an attempt to placate and pacify. Fortunately, existential therapies can promote an emancipatory stance, in a raising of consciousness. They are open to alternative ways of understanding distress, in which harmful actions can be understood as protests. The origin of a person's distress is sought in their unique response to the world that they inhabit (Deurzen, 2010).

When we are trying to understand human distress as a meaningful response to where it is that we find ourselves, self-harm is not reduced a symptom of illness. Behaviours such as self-starvation and the mortification of the body have been expressed in some religious practices. In mystical Christian traditions and in some Buddhist communities, for example, history also tells us that these practices were popularised within ancient Greek philosophy. It is possible that self-harm is more common in communities where philosophical beliefs create a sharp division between the body and the mind. Existential thinking does not support this division. Embodied being is an existential theme.

Although the impulse to harm oneself can be an isolating and intensely personal experience, it is also a form of communication. It can be an effective political move, a dramatic means of expressing our resistance to oppression. Existential practitioners will ask therefore, why it is that one person in a relationship network is feeling that impulse more than others. Why is that specific person driven to release emotional pressure by self-harming?

It is paradoxical that Socrates felt obliged to take his own life, when that is, his peers rejected his philosophy and humiliated him (Hughes, 2011). However, we do not value existential philosophers because we think they always did the right thing or lived perfect lives. We value them because they are flawed, and human like us. We attend to how they responded to the circumstances in which they found themselves. How it is that useful understandings of our human condition are revealed by this.

In therapeutic practice, it is helpful to take that not-knowing stance, as Socrates would have recommended. If someone plans to take their life, we do not know if they will act on their plan. We do not know whether they will be successful or not, whether they will survive or not. Or perhaps they will cause harm to their body, thereby making their life even more difficult to endure. If they did choose to go on living, we do not even know whether their life will become more tolerable and meaningful or not. We can only hope that it will, being open to that possibility.

5.9   If anxiety is inevitable, how do we learn to live with it?

It is understandable that we would be anxious, when we do not know what is going to happen in the future. This is a central existential theme. We might respond to our uncertainty by engaging in a detailed study of our history, seeking clues to what usually happens in given circumstances. Through these explorations, we might even find out how it is that we have arrived at our current cultural understandings of anxiety. Existential philosophy is aligned with phenomenological research, in which we question our assumptions (as explained in Section 2.3). Using this kind of deconstruction, we can ask why is that it in our current era, anxiety is thought to be a problem. Following Michel Foucault, we can engage in a kind of cultural archaeology (1966).

John Locke is a key philosopher in the development of a modern Western understanding of the self. The idea of the rational individual who is learning to function in the world can be traced back to his writings (Taylor, 1989). In those writings, he frequently recommended that we treat our children harshly, that we instil them with anxiety, so that they are motivated to learn. Anxiety is subsequently thought to be necessary for a person's development. Søren Kierkegaard agreed but qualified this with that observation of his, that it is necessary for us to be anxious in the right way (1912c).

When we are exploring our social history, we might notice that in their childhoods, our parents and our grandparents were more often subject to a strict discipline. Fashions in child-rearing change and now there is an expectation that we should be much kinder to our children. We can also feel that we should protect them from harsh realities and difficult truths. John Locke might have asked how are our children to learn, if they are not told the truth, if they do not face hardships? Perhaps our young people will grow up lacking in resilience. Many people, it seems, do struggle to tolerate their anxiety. They seek help from mental health services, asking for it to be treated and removed.

How to be anxious in the right way is a question that Rollo May took up in his clinical practice and in his writing. He makes a distinction between normal anxiety and neurotic anxiety. In his reading of what Kierkegaard was saying, May observes that a healthy anxiety will latch onto us and follow us until we turn to face it (May, 1977). Neurotic anxiety is expressed instead when we resist and refuse to face up to what it is that our concerns are telling us. His account also takes something from what Martin Heidegger says about existential guilt (1927). This is the kind of guilt we might feel if we have avoided the call of our anxiety. When we have failed to turn up; failed to live our life with courage. We can find ourselves worrying that we have not made the most of our opportunities, that we have wasted our time in diversions, distractions, and avoidances.

Existential philosophers tend to agree that if we are free of anxiety, then we are not really living. May explores psychodynamic theory, observing that we might repress our awareness of what it is that troubles us. We might displace our anxiety into phobias. We might identify with a bully who is making us anxious and become a bully ourselves. We might project our anxiety into another person and act to abuse or protect them, insisting that they are the one who is vulnerable. Learning to live with anxiety might then be about learning to manage without these maladaptive coping strategies.

Anxiety can certainly be an overwhelming and disabling emotional experience. If maladaptive coping strategies help us to function to some extent, it is understandable that we would continue to use them. However, many therapeutic approaches recommend a kind of graded exposure. We are encouraged to engage in situations which make us anxious, to gradually build our tolerance. It can be useful to be aware that the physiological changes we experience in our anxiety are not dissimilar to those of excitement. Whether an experience is exciting, or anxiety provoking, can be to some degree a matter of how we interpret what is happening for us. There is a risk, however, that we might decide that suffering is good for people, that they must push through the pain. Existential philosophy is useful when it reminds us that there is no given right way to do things. Who are we to decide whether someone else should suffer or not? In existential therapeutic practice, it is thought to be more helpful to stay with an exploration of what it is that the person is experiencing. Practitioners do not leap in to interpret or fix their client.

5.10   Are existential ideas still relevant to modern life?

Time is an existential theme, and our current era is just a moment in the flux of our complex global histories. At this point in those histories, the desire to place everything in the world in categories seems to be stronger than ever. Existentialism, as we might read in our textbooks, 'is a philosophy that was popular in the mid-twentieth century.' In this kind of categorisation, it is required that we construct the otherness of people in their different times and places. Yet we can only grasp that otherness by comparing their ways of being with our own. Existential thinking can pull us in two opposing directions. It asks us to start where we are, to consider our place in the world as the foundation of our being. At the same time, it asks us to recognise the random and absurd nature of that contingent place. It is just one way of being amongst many, with no framework for deciding which way of being is correct.

In our Western societies, with our given philosophical heritage, we continue to ask: 'how should we live?.' In our times, we are often obsessing about risk, well-being, and regulation. Now that we are aware of climate change, we can feel a greater responsibility for doing something useful and purposeful. We know that just by existing we use up resources, and we owe a debt to the planet. Some of us are also concerned about the rise of popularism in politics. The way in which this is once more propagating divisions in our societies. As we navigate pandemics, wars, economic hardships, and natural disasters, we debate our freedoms and responsibilities.

In our contemporary global culture, we continue to feel the pull of different ideologies. Some people still want the protection of strong leaders. Some still seek the guidance of clear ethical or religious codes. Others want more freedom, although perhaps only some of them are willing to accept the personal responsibilities that come with that. These ongoing conflicts continue to erupt into violence and oppression, people continue to suffer. There are some changes, most evident in the influence of technology, but we face the same existential dilemmas as the people that came before us.

Martin Heidegger, in his later work, observes how the advance of technology turns aspects of our world into resources, and people can also become commodities. In the rationalised instrumentalism of commercial economics, people are a 'standing-reserve,' a resource waiting to be used (Heidegger, 1977). It can make us anxious to be inactive, waiting to be picked up, used, then put down again. Heidegger's solution was to go off on his own and spend time in a hut in the forest. Should we follow his example? We could travel now to an unspoilt wilderness, only to find a coachload of other tourists have arrived just before us. For some of us, when we try to forge our independence and freedom, there are strong leaders who will pull us back into line. Yet standing out as an individual is also difficult in less restricted lives, when that is, we find that we are still in the crowd following the latest trend.

Many contemporary theorists, who could be read as expressing existentialist principles, do not use that term. The question of 'what is it like to be a person?' is now addressed most often by academics who refer to their work as phenomenological. This is aligned closely with questions that are asked by psychological therapists. These existential questions have thereby escaped. We find that the ideas existential theorists explore are roaming free in our conversations and our ways of being. We now know, for example, what it is to have an existential crisis, to have a disputed identity, and to be objectified.

It seems that now, with the constant babble of social media, no life goes unexamined. The look that Jean-Paul Sartre wrote about decades ago is now watching us constantly through security cameras. Many people enthusiastically embrace this surveillance, posting pictures of themselves, recording their location, and who it is that they are meeting. Anyone can see how they are spending their time and money. We are invited to judge whether they are 'living their best life' or not. In these displays, people are resisting the positioning of others, trying to establish a positive identity.

Existential philosophy has become more widely read, probably because it is a kind of academic thinking that addresses concerns which we all share. We are all embodied social people seeking meaning. The conversation has grown and extended through cross-cultural encounters, with an expansion of consciousness, opening to different voices. It is a part of the debates which moved us from structuralism to poststructuralism and into postmodernism. We attend much more now to how we construct our versions of the truth, through our use of language.

Trends come and go but we continue to struggle with the same given aspects of our existence. Academic debates can give the impression that new ideas are being developed, while established theory fades away. We try to increase our social value by aligning with the latest ideas. However, we must be careful when we engage in these arguments, when we do not own the words that we are speaking. Words do not sprout fresh and pure from our mouths; they have been in many other mouths before ours. We are free to decide that existential philosophers are something to do with the past. We can conclude that their words are no longer meaningful for us. However, there is a sense in which today, we can consider questions of what is meaningful for us, only because of the debates that those philosophers initiated.

Further reading

Abram, D. (1996). *The Spell of the Sensuous: Perception and Language in a More-Than-Human World.* Vintage Books.

Bakewell, S. (2017). *At the Existential Café: Freedom, Being & Apricot Cocktails.* Penguin-Random House.

Goodman, W. (2022). *Toxic Positivity: Keeping It Real in a World Obsessed with Being Happy.* Tarcher Perigee.

Okakura, K. (1906: 2012). *The Book of Tea.* Watchmaker Publishing.

Yalom, I. (1989). *Love's Executioner and Other Tales of Psychotherapy.* Harper Perennial.

References

Bakewell, S. (2017). *At the Existential Café: Freedom, Being & Apricot Cocktails.* Penguin-Random House.

Beauvoir, S. de (1949). *The Second Sex* (C. Borde & S. Malovany-Chevallier, trans.). Random House (2009).

Biko, S. (1978). *I Write What I Like: Selected Writings.* University of Chicago Press (2002).

Binswanger, L. (1958). The case of Ellen West (W.M. Mendel & J. Lyons, trans.). In R. May, E. Angel, & H.F. Ellenberger (Eds.), *Existence: A New Dimension in Psychiatry and Psychology.* Basic Books, 237–364.

Binswanger, L. (1963). *Being-in-the-World: Selected Papers of Ludwick Binswanger* (J. Needleman, trans.). Souvenir Press (1975).

Blackwell, D. (2009). Mortality and meaning in refugee survivors of torture and organized violence. In L. Barnett (Ed.), *When Death Enters the Therapeutic Space: Existential Perspectives in Psychotherapy and Counselling.* Routledge, 105–116.

Buber, M. (1937). *I and Thou* (S. Verlag, trans.). Bloomsbury Academic (2013).

Campo, J.V. (2009). Suicide prevention: Time for 'zero tolerance.' *Current Opinion in Pediatrics, 21*(5), 611–612.

Camus, A. (1942). *The Stranger* (M. Ward, trans.). Vintage Books (1989).

Camus, A. (1955). *The Myth of Sisyphus and Other Essays* (J. O'Brien, trans.). Vintage Books (1991).

Carel, H. (2016). *Phenomenology of Illness.* Oxford University Press.

Derrida, J. (1976). *Of Grammatology* (G.C. Spivak, trans.). The Johns Hopkins University Press.

Deurzen, E. van (2010). *Everyday Mysteries: A Handbook of Existential Psychotherapy, Second Edition.* Routledge.

Deurzen, E. van, & Arnold-Baker, C. (2018). *Existential Therapy: Distinctive Features.* Routledge.

Eger, E. (2017). *The Choice.* London: Rider.

Fanon, F. (1967). *Black Skin, White Masks.* Grove Press.

Foucault, M. (1966). *The Order of Things: An Archaeology of the Human Sciences.* Vintage Books (1970).

Frankl, V.E. (1946). *Man's Search for Meaning.* Ebury (2004).

Heidegger, M. (1927). *Being and Time* (J. Macquarrie & E. Robinson, trans.). Harper & Row (1962).

Heidegger, M. (1977). *The Question Concerning Technology and Other Essays* (W. Lovitt, trans.). Harper & Row.

Hughes, B. (2011). *The Hemlock Cup: Socrates, Athens and the Search for the Good Life.* Jonathan Cape.

Jaspers, K. (1932). *Philosophy, Vol. 2: Existential Elucidation* (E.B. Ashton, trans.). The University of Chicago Press (1970).

Joseph, S. (2012). *What Doesn't Kill Us: The New Psychology of Posttraumatic Growth.* Piatkus Little Brown.

Kant, I. (1786). Metaphysical foundations of natural science. In H. Allison & P. Heath (Eds.) (G. Hatfield & M. Friedman, trans.). *Theoretical Philosophy after 1781* (The Cambridge Edition of the Works of Immanuel Kant). Cambridge University Press (2002), 171–270.

Kierkegaard, S. (1912a). The concept of irony, with continual reference to Socrates. In H.V. Hong & E.H. Hong (Eds.), *The Essential Kierkegaard.* Princeton University Press (2000), 20–36.

Kierkegaard, S. (1912b). The sickness unto death. In H.V. Hong & E.H. Hong (Eds.), *The Essential Kierkegaard.* Princeton University Press (2000), 350–372.

Kierkegaard, S. (1912c). The concept of anxiety. In H.V. Hong & E.H. Hong (Eds.), *The Essential Kierkegaard.* Princeton University Press (2000), 138–155.

Macintyre, A. (2006). *Edith Stein; A Philosophical Prologue.* Continuum.

May, R. (1977). *The Meaning of Anxiety.* W. W. Norton (2015).

Merleau-Ponty, M. (1945). *The Phenomenology of Perception* (C. Smith, trans.). Routledge (1962).

Minkowski, E. (1933). *Lived Time: Phenomenological and Psychopathological Studies* (N. Metzel, trans.). Northwestern University Press (2019).

Okakura, K. (1906). *The Book of Tea.* Watchmaker Publishing (2012).

Orr, J. (2014). 'Being and timelessness' Edith Stein's critique of Heideggerian temporality. *Modern Theology*, *30*(1), 114–131.

Ricoeur, P. (1981). *Hermeneutics and the Human Sciences* (J.B. Thompson, trans.). Cambridge University Press.

Sartre, J-P. (1943). *Being and Nothingness* (H. Barnes, trans.). Washington Square Press (1984).

Sartre, J-P. (1972). *Sketch for a Theory of Emotions* (P. Maire, trans.). Methuen.

Seymour-Jones, C. (2009). *A Dangerous Liaison: A Revelatory New Biography of Simone de Beauvoir and Jean-Paul Sartre.* Abrams.

Stein, E. (1921). *On the Problem of Empathy: The Collected Works of Edith Stein* (W. Stein, trans.). ICS Publications (1989).

Stein, E. (1922). *Philosophy of Psychology and the Humanities* (M.C. Baseheart & M. Sawicki, trans.). ICS Publication (2000).

Stein, E. (1950). *Martin Heidegger's Existential Philosophy* (M. Lebech, trans.). Maynooth Philosophical Papers (2006).

Stolorow, R.D. (2007). *Trauma and Human Existence: Autobiographical, Psychoanalytic and Philosophical Reflections.* The Analytic Press.

Taylor, C. (1989). *Sources of the Self: The Making of Modern Identity.* Harvard University Press.

Tedeschi, R.G., Park, C.L., & Calhoun, L.G. (1998). *Posttraumatic Growth: Positive Transformations in the Aftermath of Crisis.* Lawrence Erlbaum.

Tillich, P. (2014). *The Courage to Be* (Third Edition). Yale University Press.

Wang, Y.N. (2015). Authenticity and relationship satisfaction: Two distinct ways of directing power to self-esteem. *PLoS ONE, 10*(12), e0146050. https://doi.org/10.1371/journal.pone.0146050

Yalom, I.D. (1980). *Existential Psychotherapy.* Basic Books.

Conclusion

Claire Arnold-Baker

The primary task of philosophy is to question what we know about life and existence. It requires philosophers to be curious and naïve, open and receptive to new possibilities and perspectives. Of course, this way of approaching the world is not just restricted to the domain of those who have studied philosophy and have made it their life's work. As Sartre and Beauvoir have argued (see Part 1.1), existential philosophy can, and should, be practiced by all and applied in everyday situations. The *love of wisdom*, which is at the heart of philosophy, can be shared by everyone. It is rather apt then, that this book is structured around 50 questions that are frequently asked by people who are curious about the existential approach, whether they are prospective trainees, clients, or people who are drawn to existential themes and ideas.

It is hard to do justice to such a wide academic and therapeutic discipline, which spans many centuries of thinkers and practitioners in such a short space. But we hope that the answers to the questions posed here have prompted you to read further and has ignited a desire to explore beyond the pages of this book.

The existential approach to therapy is a truly unique approach and the only therapeutic approach that is based entirely on philosophy. As you will have seen throughout the book its philosophical basis gives a different perspective on the struggles we

DOI: 10.4324/9781003355700-7

face as human beings. Preferring to see these struggles as problems in living rather than problems of the psyche. This different orientation means that clients feel more empowered in how they can become active agents in their lives rather than feeling at the mercy of circumstance, with a label which can limit and determine them. This non-pathologising approach is often seen as a welcome antidote to a more restrictive medical model of mental distress. The existential approach also highlights how life is a struggle for everyone and that we must all find a path through the limitations of our existence. But rather than being an overly pessimistic approach, these struggles are conceptualised as challenges that can lead to growth and wisdom and better ways of living.

People who come to complete existential training often say how much the existential approach resonates with them. They feel a connection with the philosophical ideas and the way these ideas conceptualise the world. It is not an easy approach to learn as although Sartre and Beauvoir believed that existentialism should be an applied philosophy, it was never written as a particular method. In fact, it has been argued that there are as many ways to do existential therapy as there are existential therapists. The first stage in learning how to work existentially is for the trainee to immerse themselves in the philosophy and to begin applying it to their own lives. Trainees need to really *live* the philosophy as it is only through their own relationship with existential ideas that they can begin to apply them to other people. These elements of practice have been described in further detail in Parts 2 and 3 of this book.

In this age of hyper-connectivity, of the internet and social media, we have become more disconnected from ourselves, others, the world around us, and our planet. There has been an increase in the rates of mental disorders for 17–19 year olds from 17.4% in 2021 to 25.7% in 2022 (NHS Digital, 2022). The World Health Organization (WHO) have also reported a 13% increase in mental health conditions worldwide in the last decade (WHO, 2023). Simply put: our way of living is causing us distress. An existential approach is not necessarily going to provide an answer to all of life's problems, as Deurzen-Smith states 'there is no blueprint for living'(1988), but it does encourage people to shake off the shackles of living in an automated way where they sleepwalk through life, existing and not really living. Existential philosophy and therapy therefore inspires people to start thinking deeply about their lives, to ask themselves questions about the way they are living: what is important in their lives, what do they value, and how can they find meaning and purpose? The answers can only be found within the individual themselves, but an existential therapist can guide and question, and open up new perspectives that did not seem possible or which were just not available before. What is needed at this current time is an existential awakening. Existentialism and the existential therapeutic approach are well suited to providing a framework to help people make sense of their experiences, to move forward through times of crisis and transition and to reconnect with what is important: relationships – our relationship with ourselves, with other people, and with our world. We hope that this book will be the start of this journey of discovery.

References

Deurzen-Smith, E. van (1988). *Existential Counselling in Practice*. Sage.

NHS Digital (2022). *Rate of Mental Disorders among 17 to 19 Year Olds Increased in 2022.* Retrieved on 31 January 2023, from: https://digital.nhs.uk/news/2022/rate-of-mental-disorders-among-17-to-19-year-olds-increased-in-2022-new-report-shows

World Health Organization (WHO) (2023). *Mental Health.* Retrieved on 31 January 2023, from: www.who.int/health-topics/mental-health

Index

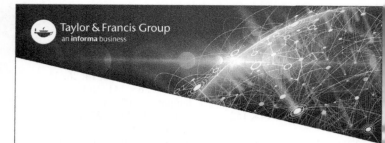